Learning and Mental Health in the School

Prepared by the ASCD 1966 Yearbook Committee

Edited by
Walter B. Waetjen, Chairman of the Yearbook Committee
and
Robert R. Leeper, Editor, ASCD Publications

Andrew S. Thomas Memorial Library
MORRIS HARVEY COLLEGE, CHARLESTON, W. VA.

Association for Supervision and Curriculum Development, NEA
1201 Sixteenth Street, N.W.
Washington, D.C. 20036

370.58
As78y
1966

Copyright © 1966 by the

Association for Supervision and Curriculum Development, NEA
1201 Sixteenth Street, N.W., Washington, D.C. 20036

Price $5.00

Library of Congress Catalog Card Number: 44-6213

Contents

Foreword   **v**
Galen Saylor

Acknowledgments   vii

About Learning and Mental Health:
An Introduction   **1**
Walter B. Waetjen

1   Mutuality of Effective Functioning and School Experiences   **9**
James Raths

2   The Achievement of Competency   **23**
Eli M. Bower

3   New Conceptions of Children's Learning and Development   **49**
Ira J. Gordon

4   A Cognitive Field Theory of Learning   **77**
Donald Snygg

5   Self-Actualization:
    A New Focus for Education   **99**
        Elizabeth Monroe Drews

6   Learning and Becoming—
    New Meanings to Teachers   **127**
        Marie M. Hughes

7   The School and the Ego
    as Information Processors   **147**
        Walter B. Waetjen and Kenneth C. Weisbrod

    The ASCD 1966 Yearbook Committee and Contributors   **170**

    ASCD Executive Committee   **171**

    ASCD Board of Directors   **171**

    ASCD Headquarters Staff   **174**

Foreword

Learning and Mental Health in the School is a most stimulating, helpful and exciting book. The volume is stimulating in that it is a masterful treatment of the subject of mental health and its relationship to the learning process. It is helpful in that it will provide educators in all positions of responsibility—teachers, supervisors, curriculum coordinators, curriculum directors, principals, and superintendents of schools—a great many ideas and concepts that should guide educational practice and planning. The book is exciting because it dramatically brings together a large body of new concepts, new research, and new theories about the learning process and mental health that have for some time now been proposed and propounded by some of our more forward-looking researchers and theorists in the field of human growth and development.

Learning and Mental Health in the School is the fourth of an ASCD series of yearbooks on the general subject of mental health and personal development in its various social, emotional and intellectual aspects. These four volumes constitute an outstanding contribution to the literature on these topics. The 1940 Yearbook, *Mental Health in the Classroom* (prepared by one of our two predecessor organizations), was an outstanding early work that provided guidance for the teacher in working with children so that the mental health of each pupil was enhanced. The 1950 Yearbook, *Fostering Mental Health in Our Schools*, was highly acclaimed by the profession and extensively used in college classrooms throughout the country in the study of ego development, mental health, and personality development of pupils. The 1962 Yearbook, *Perceiving, Behaving, Becoming: A New Focus for Education*, is also accepted by the profession as an outstanding contribution to the literature. It seems rather obvious to all who have read advance copies of *Learning and Mental Health in the School*, that this volume, too, will be enthusiastically acclaimed by the educators.

Each chapter of the yearbook is an exciting adventure for the reader. The focus of each chapter is clear; the theories, points of view, and rationale for such points of view, together with references to supporting research data where pertinent, are forcefully stated and logically organized. Each chapter is a scholarly piece of writing and an outstanding contribution to that specific topic. The book is worthy of ASCD, and ASCD is worthy of the book. It constitutes an emphatic rejection of a mechanistic, rigid, inflexible, dehumanized kind of psychology of human growth and development and of the learning process that has characterized far too much of our professional literature in recent years.

The Yearbook Committee views mental health as a process and hence as an aspect of all experience situations in the school. Living and learning are not a discrete series of isolated events or experiences. Mental health is the result of the totality of living and learning and not merely supplementary bits of experience that are not an integral part of the classroom learning situation itself. The emphasis on individual freedom, on the necessity of acting in harmony with reality, on acceptance and challenge constitutes an exciting plan of action for teachers and curriculum workers in our schools. The whole educational process is viewed in broad scope, not simply as the mastery of a prescribed body of knowledge but rather as a competency to deal with the world as it exists or might exist. And the concluding chapter of the yearbook points out the significance of all of these reality-related approaches to learning and mental health for curriculum planning and teaching.

In light of the outstanding merits of these contributions, chapter by chapter, it is apparent that all members of the Association for Supervision and Curriculum Development and, in fact, all members of the profession who are really concerned about what happens to boys and girls owe a great debt of gratitude to the ASCD 1966 Yearbook Committee. It is indeed my pleasure and privilege to express to the members of this Committee on behalf of the Board of Directors, the Executive Committee, and the total membership of the Association our highest and most lavish appreciation for this unselfish effort in helping all of us better to guide the wholesome development of every boy and girl progressing through the years of formal schooling in this country.

November 1965 GALEN SAYLOR, *President,*
Association for Supervision
and Curriculum Development

Acknowledgments

THE ASSOCIATION would like to express special appreciation to William G. Hollister, M.D., Professor of Community Psychiatry, Department of Psychiatry, University of North Carolina Medical School, for his origination of the idea for this yearbook, and to the National Institute of Mental Health for its support, jointly with ASCD, of the Seminar which met on May 6, 1963, in Washington, D.C., the deliberations of which served as the basis for the volume. Participants in that meeting who contributed greatly to the original planning for this yearbook were: Walter B. Waetjen, Eli M. Bower, Robert J. Havighurst, Paul R. Klohr, Norman Reider, Anatol Rapoport, Ralph W. Tyler, Fritz Redl, Arno A. Bellack, Gardner Murphy and Margaret Gill.

Special acknowledgment is made to the members of the Yearbook Committee who also wrote the several chapters of the volume and served as readers and critics of the book in its entirety. Walter B. Waetjen, Yearbook Committee Chairman, and Robert R. Leeper, Editor, ASCD Publications, edited the manuscript in its final form. Technical production of the book was handled by Karen L. Farr, Editorial Assistant, under the supervision of Ruth P. Ely, Editorial Associate.

About Learning and Mental Health: An Introduction

Walter B. Waetjen

THIS yearbook is about learning and mental health. At first blush a person might think that there is no possible reason why such a volume should be produced. Behind such a thought would be the idea that for several centuries teachers have been concerned about the learning of their pupils. Some would aver that for at least a decade teachers have been concerned about the mental health of those whom they teach. The Yearbook Committee that has planned and written this volume could only agree with these points of view. Yet if members of the Committee had dismissed the issue without further thought, then there would have been no reason for proceeding with this yearbook.

Even a moment's reflection on the matter of learning brings to mind that the teacher is placed in a dilemma on this subject. For if a teacher is to help a pupil to learn, this means that the teacher must do something about his teaching. But what? Should he arrange his subject matter differently? Should he present it differently? Should he give the pupils more, or less, responsibility for planning the learning activities? Or should the teacher do all of these things?

To compound the dilemma, some of the learning theories to which most teachers subscribe require close scrutiny. The theories or laws of learning that many teachers believe in (if they believe in any) are based on data obtained using animals as subjects. If the subjects were human beings, then they, like the animals, were in highly controlled unclassroom-like situations. As a consequence, the findings are only remotely related to what the teacher experiences in the classroom. It seems strange that, in a society that does so much experimentation in psychological processes, we have a rather meager psychology of individual differences that may be utilized by the teacher. Yet these are observations that have relevance only to learning—what about mental health?

By virtue of the teacher education process, mental health is not seen as a reality by either preservice or in-service teachers. This is not to say that they do not see some merit in fostering mental health in our schools, for indeed they do. Yet it seems that most teachers see mental health as something apart from teaching. Counseling, which is not part of the teaching act, would be perceived by teachers as a mental health function of the school. Likewise, they would view the activities of the school psychologist and the school social worker as the school's role in the development of better mental health. One cannot deny that these are mental health functions of the school, but it should be recognized that these functions are quite distinct from what occurs in the elementary school classroom, the algebra class, the chemistry class, or the civics class.

Some directors of curriculum would rise in hot protest against the previous statement and point with conviction to the fact that mental health is highly central to the teaching activity in their school system. Typically, in these cases the curriculum director is likely to produce a course of study or a curriculum unit that is taught at some given grade. Or perhaps the same type of unit with modification is taught at several different grade levels. Logic in such an approach seems to be that mental health is so important that we must make of it a highly cognitive activity. In this instance mental health is seen as a *thing* to be taught rather than as a *process* to be engaged in.

These two views of mental health have been disavowed by the Yearbook Committee. To our minds mental health is not something out of which one makes a curriculum unit but rather it is something that occurs in the context of the moment-to-moment discourse and interaction between pupils and teachers in classrooms. We have taken the position that there are potentialities for influencing mental health in teaching the skills and understandings necessary to cope with the environment, the skills of communication, the ways of identifying and solving problems rationally, and the basic requirements needed for pursuing a vocation. Viewed in this way, mental health is a process and processes usually have a product. In this case the product is the competent person, a term that will be used throughout the context of this yearbook.

Learning and Mental Health in the School

To place blame on teachers for not doing more about mental health and learning of pupils would be unfair. It may be that there is a standardization of teaching practices and attitudes in teachers. Yet, this may be caused by the fact that teachers are so surrounded by regulations and requirements and notions about teaching and learning that they stultify their teaching capacity and damage their trust in themselves. Teaching, to be good, must have large elements of creativity and spontaneity— neither of which elements can long survive in an atmosphere in which conformity to senseless regulations plays a dominant part. In such an atmosphere a teacher himself cannot learn and he in turn has difficulty teaching in such a way that his pupils can learn. The consequence is that pupils have difficulty in becoming competent persons.

In the pages to follow it will become readily apparent to the reader that the writers have subscribed to a certain kind of education. The education to which we have subscribed has one great and overarching purpose and that is the achievement of individual freedom. We do not use the words "individual freedom" in the way that they might be used by an aspirant to political office. In that context the words are often vague and rather meaningless. Nor does individual freedom mean just doing whatever one likes. Freedom is never free, there is always some price to pay. As will be pointed out in all of the chapters that ensue, the price that the mentally healthy, learning-oriented pupil pays for his freedom in the classroom is that he accepts the responsibility for his acts.

Pupils are only truly free when they are acting in accordance with reality. That is, with events, things and people as they really are. They are bound and unfree to the extent to which they are incapable of seeing things as they really are. Thus, freedom has nothing to do with license, but it has a great deal to do with being sufficiently aware of ourselves and sufficiently aware of our feelings and thinking to be able to see and respond to things as they are. It takes only a moment's reflection, then, to see that education needs to concern itself with the liberation of the individual.

It is only the pupil who is free who can begin to see things as they really are and who can begin to live and act in harmony with the reality principle rather than principles of personal defensiveness. Of course, one could easily misinterpret the statement to the extent of believing that this yearbook holds curriculum content to be unimportant. This would be a most unfortunate interpretation, for actually we hold the view that curriculum content, if taught properly, can indeed be a liberating force for all pupils. This same curriculum content could enable a youngster not only to discover reality, but to test it; and, the curriculum content would indeed give pupils a lever on the world, as it properly should.

Education is harmful to the extent to which it makes independent thinking difficult and to the degree to which it makes pupils distrust their own experience. If education is dominated by the belief that the accumulation of knowledge is valuable in itself, then we are only playing party to moving our society down the path of conformity and a spectacular lack of creativity and inventiveness. Significant learning and mental health start with questions that spring out of real life and that are forced upon us by pressure of events. This kind of learning is necessarily disciplined by objective fact. There is practically no value whatever in knowing things just for the sake of knowing them and nothing more.

The search for knowledge is either a search for that which has significance for human behavior or it is a relapse into unreality. The contents of Chapters 5 and 6 should make it crystal clear that what we are advocating can occur in a classroom in which there is a curriculum and in which the teacher accepts responsibility for "structuring" the classroom activities. So much of the so-called academic life, especially college academic life, has around it an aura of futility and barrenness because it has so little significance to and for the individual learner. If a learner has freedom, with its attendant responsibilities in the classroom, all other forms of learning necessary for living in our contemporary world come more easily to him—for learning comes more easily to one who is unrestricted intellectually.

It is in school that a pupil can see his own small world of home from the outside and can begin to make his independent judgments of parents and their demands. School can provide a child with an opportunity for self-discovery. At school he is not imprisoned in the kind of personality that his parents have come to accept as his. At school he can experiment with new roles and thus find out who he really is and what he is capable of. But this kind of "role rehearsal" occurs best when the teacher makes provision for it. He does not rely upon chance occurrences. The school can encourage independence of thinking and create an atmosphere in which every belief is questioned. In short, school can become a place in which the doubt is prized. School can be a place where a pupil can be discontented with things as they are without fearing reprisal. Of course, the discontentment of the pupil must be expressed in ways that are socially acceptable and which lead to some constructive social action on his part. In this yearbook we have tried to point out that our schools can become places where a pupil learns the difference between experiencing and the explaining of experiences.

Introduction 5

Preview of the Yearbook

A quick glance through this book will reveal that each chapter is preceded by a brief discussion of the major ideas in the chapter that follows. In this brief discussion, each author has presented his main points with the hope that they will serve to map the intellectual territory to be covered by the reader. Thus the reader may anticipate and be able to relate the material in the chapter. This arrangement was intended also as a good teaching procedure. When major concepts are presented in advance, a learner can relate the more minor facts, principles and generalizations to these major concepts. We encourage the reader to make full use of these brief discussions. As a matter of fact, it would be well before reading anything else in the yearbook, to read each one of these one-page discussions in serial order. This will give the reader a concise and accurate summary of the total volume. Even though this course of action is open to the reader, there is another alternative and that is a discussion of the rationale or point of view which binds the book together.

Of course, there was a problem central to the yearbook. The problem was that while both mental health and learning are of utmost importance, how do we plan a curriculum that recognizes and promotes growth of each pupil in both of these areas? The advantages, difficulties and social implications of this dilemma are discussed. However, in the discussion two key words seem to emerge. These words are *acceptance* and *challenge*. Acceptance refers to pupils' thoughts and feelings, while challenge refers to the pupils' challenging of the generalizations and the concepts that are inherent in the structure of knowledge in the curriculum. These points are made clear in Chapter 1.

There can be little doubt that educators are people who are operationally oriented. They are much more eager to do things than they are to reflect on ideas. A society needs doers, but it is also true that the doers need some point of view or theory on which they can base their action. It was with this in mind that the Yearbook Committee organized Chapters 2, 3, and 4. It was our belief that nothing is so practical as a good theory. Chapter 2 is a discussion of mental health from the point of view of the qualities that one needs in order to be able to function competently. These qualities are the ability to work, to play and to love. The importance of these qualities and their effect on learning is developed.

Chapter 3 is a reexamination and a comparison of some of the research evidence that has to do with the development, learning and motivation of human beings. These research findings have to do with physical, social and emotional development and their impact on learning and motivation. A central concept of the chapter is that a human being is a unified system in the sense that he is continually organizing all of the information that he receives both from within himself and from his environment.

Chapter 4 gives emphasis to the inadequacy of some of our "notions" about learning, and also about reinforcement theories of learning as guides to teachers' action in the classroom. As an alternative there is proposed a cognitive field theory of learning which provides a more realistic basis for instructional planning and evaluation and for teachers' understanding and dealing with the problems of individual pupils.

If Chapters 2, 3, and 4 constitute the more theoretical part of the Yearbook, then by the same token Chapters 5 and 6 are oriented more toward the "how-to-do-it." Yet the authors of these chapters protest such a cookbook description and are quick to point out that a teacher must find his unique modes of translating the theory into action. Their chapters, then, are a description of how a few teachers put into effect some of the points which have been discussed in earlier chapters.

The final chapter has to do with the common denominator of all the other chapters. We refer, of course, to the concept of information. Information may be derived from a person's internal bodily processes, such as pain or emotion; it has to do with the content of the curriculum; it has to do with the way in which a teacher gently admonishes a pupil; and, it has to do with the myriad of communications that go on within a school. The flow of information within a school, as well as within a person when he learns, is of importance to the effective functioning of either the person or the school. The chapter offers to educators a novel way of viewing and appraising those functions that are carried on in schools by administrators, teachers, pupils and the various people who perform the support services.

The yearbook has three distinct emphases, the pupil, the teacher and the curriculum. The forces acting upon and within the learner emerged as central considerations in the yearbook. Likewise, the importance of the teacher's acts in fostering both mental health and learning must be considered along with pupil forces. The curriculum was seen as highly critical in the total development of pupils; for the facts, concepts and generalizations embodied in the curriculum potentially give to the learner a way of testing reality and provide him with various levers which he may use to make his way more effectively in the world. More important, the yearbook puts emphasis on how these three forces may be orchestrated in such a way as to produce a person who is highly adept at learning, is exquisitely sensitive to the environment about him, is compassionate toward his fellow man and can manage stress. From our point of view this is a description of the competent person.

Mutuality of Effective Functioning and School Experiences

Most educators agree that concerns for the child and for the curriculum are met only as the characteristics of both are known, prized and preserved. The question is how to do just that—plan a course of study that promotes growth in both areas.

As teachers provide an environment that accepts children's feelings and thoughts *and* challenges concepts and generalizations contained in the curriculum or courses of study, they may demonstrate the mutuality of school learnings and effective functioning.

1

Mutuality of Effective Functioning and School Experiences

James Raths

WHILE the practice of education in the public schools can be characterized accurately as aphilosophical, many teachers, supervisors, and curriculum workers generally agree with John Dewey's formulations regarding the importance of the child *and* the curriculum (6). It is clear to most educators that concerns for the child and for subject matter are met only as the characteristics of both are known, prized and preserved. The problem that has plagued curriculum workers and teachers for centuries is how to do just that—plan a course of study based on knowledge of children *and* subject matter. This dilemma has been well summarized by Lawrence Kubie: "How can we equip the child with the facts and the tools which he will need in life, without interfering with the freedom with which he will be able to use them after he has acquired them?" (14). Too often, curriculum formulations place too much value at one end or the other of the curriculum-child continuum.

For example, the *New York Times Magazine* reported recent studies indicating that first graders could learn the principles of economics (9). The headline of the article included the caption: "Two-year-olds are very smart—Extremely young children can be taught almost any subject." The article was predictively quite supportive of the intentions reflected in these studies. It is difficult not to admire the work of university scholars in developing elementary school curriculum materials, yet an important consideration seems missing from their reports and pronouncements. While first grade children apparently can be taught any subject, the question remains what *should* elementary school children be learning? What learnings promote the realization of human potential?

Some curriculum workers take a different view. Children should study in areas that are of concern to them—not in areas of concern to the teacher or the university scholars. Such a curriculum is established when curriculum workers are able to "step down from the rostrum of the expert and look at the world through the eyes of the learner" (2). The teacher's function is to guide the student toward the formulation of a problem. "But it must be the pupil's problem and one which really challenges him, not a problem which concerns only a teacher or an expert" (2).

It would be unfair to conclude that these instances exemplify persons not concerned with the welfare of the child, in the first case, or persons not concerned with the curriculum content in the other. Yet these cases do illustrate the persistence and ubiquity of the problem that is perplexing educators: "The child and the curriculum?" Again, as Kubie sees it:

> We have learned that both input-overload through the excessive use of grill and drill, and input-overload through excessive permissiveness may tumble the learner into precisely the same abyss of paralysis and ignorance. Out of them can emerge either that special form of idiot-savant, the man who is a scholar in his field but humanly speaking an ignoramus . . . or alternatively and at the other end of the pole . . . the factually uncluttered mind, the master of nothing, free of burden of facts but equally under the dominion of his own neurosis (14).

This yearbook is an attempt to reexamine this question in the light of the newer conceptions of the child and the curriculum. It intends to reaffirm the importance of both and their mutuality. The question that the Yearbook Committee has posed is essentially as follows: What is the relationship between curriculum experiences that youngsters receive in schools and the promotion of their effective functioning? The next section of the chapter is an attempt to elaborate the committee's view as to the meaning of the phrase "effective functioning."

What Is Effective Functioning?

Despite Jahoda's (13) warning to the contrary, it is perhaps easiest to discuss symptoms of illness rather than to outline the manifestations of good health. Analogously, effective functioning can be defined negatively. A person is not functioning effectively when he manifests the symptoms of credulity, escapism, dependence and other forms of rigidity that block individual growth in both the intellectual and the emotional spheres. These signs of illness, unlike narcotic addiction, alcoholism and cancer, are diseases that seem to fall primarily within the jurisdiction of schools and teachers. They are found universally in American communities, schools, neighborhoods and homes. These symptoms manifest themselves in rather subtle ways—not in the assassination of a President but in the condoning of violence in handling the "integration problem"; not in the blatant cheating on quiz shows but in the apathetic views toward the cribbing scandals at our military academies; not in the killing of civil rights workers in Mississippi but in the overlooking of the killings as "proper treatments for 'outsiders.' " Such illnesses become manifest when people cite the Bible to denounce the Jews, when teachers feel comfortable with autocratic administrators, when more people go to the horse races on a given day than vote in a primary election. Clearly, credulity, dependence and escapism are major illnesses in our society and very little is being done in our schools to cope with such illnesses.

Yet the absence of disease must be considered only a necessary and not a sufficient criterion for health. What are some positive aspects of an effectively functioning person? Essentially, the Yearbook Committee sees an effectively functioning person in terms of his relation to reality.[1] This relationship is manifest in a person's feelings of autonomy, perceptions of reality, and competency.

Feelings of Autonomy

This aspect of effective functioning stresses the notion that a person is an active agent in his environment rather than a purely reactive one. Seen in the context of decision making, a person has a sense that his fate can be altered by his decisions to act, to speak, to petition, to picket or to remain silent. He does not always have to surrender his destiny to the whims of big government, to a powerful superintendent, or to society. In this sense, such a person has a feeling of power in dealing with his environment. He feels somewhat confident in his own answers to the important questions of the day and, without feelings of threat, can continue to test his answers with a healthy prizing of the doubt.

Perceptions of Reality

The need to test answers implies that, to be able to function effectively, a person's perceptions must be relatively free from need-distor-

---

[1] The author acknowledges an intellectual debt to Marie Jahoda and her work, *Current Concepts of Positive Mental Health* (13).

tion. Mental health specialists have felt for many years that "correct" reality perception is a valid indicator of the effective functioning of an individual. However, the word "correct" need not connote that there is one and only one correct perception. Rather, it suggests that however a person perceives the world, there must be some data available to him that serve to support his perceptions. This dimension implies an openness to experience and a tolerance for instances that run counter to currently held beliefs and positions.

Competency

Finally, a person who is committed to testing his beliefs against perceptions of reality must have competency associated with the understanding of reality and with ways of inquiring into it. Modes of testing ideas of reality—research, analysis and inquiry—are important and crucial skills for the effectively functioning person. These are skills that are learned and that can be taught. A person who is able to discriminate between the relevant and irrelevant; between the facts and assumptions of an argument; and between current explanations and facts is demonstrating his competency to deal with reality in a way that complements and supports attitudes of autonomy.

In addition, as a person is skilled in dealing with his environment and in understanding the forces acting upon him, he is more likely to feel powerful and effective. Nothing is more bewildering or more likely to lead to feelings of powerlessness than ignorance. In this light, competency is an important aspect of effective functioning. It is the committee's position that a person with these attributes is able to function effectively in almost any role he is called upon to play—father, son, student, teacher, leader or follower. Such a person is free to maximize his potential for developing into the kind of person he is able to become.

What Is the Current Relationship Between School Experiences and Effective Functioning?

Current Status

Let us assume that school experiences, implementing a curriculum aimed at fostering effective functioning as already described, would be reflected at the very least in the interest patterns, values and beliefs of students. What patterns are reflected in the attitudes of American students? A historical review of education in the United States cannot help but impress the reader with the notion that American educators have assumed for some time that the central role of schools was and is to free individuals to develop their own potentialities.

It is equally clear that school leaders have consistently made an assumption that knowledge and skills mastered by students would go a long way to guarantee the accomplishment of the school's goal. In this spirit, the Old Deluder Satan Act of 1647 was passed to establish public schooling on this continent. The purpose of this act was to arm the youth of colonial Massachusetts with skills of reading and writing so that Satan, in the guise of Sophists and false-teachers, could not easily steer children away from the truth of the Bible. It was reasoned, apparently, that with reading skills, each child could find the truth for himself without having to depend upon the intermediary offices of the minister who may be elsewhere at a time of crisis or temptation when he is needed most. Whether knowing how to read led to an increased measure of devout behavior and to more frequent reliance on the Bible as a source of strength against temptations and evil is not clear at this time. From what we know today, we would doubt that such an increase took place.

Jacob (12), after a survey of many researches, found "no specific curricular pattern of general education, no model syllabus for a basic social science course, no pedigree of instructor and no wizardry of instructional method which should be patented for its impact on the values of youth." He added that evidently "the impetus to change (values) does not come from the formal educative process." Jacob certainly publicized the idea that values were not being developed in the schools of America, at least at the collegiate levels.

Concerning the high schools, the Regents Inquiry, reported in 1938, gave evidence that boys and girls who do not go on to higher education abandon many of the activities that secondary schools tried to emphasize as valuable. "Left to their own devices, most young people cease to read serious books and articles of good fiction; they seldom listen to the best music; they study as a means of preparing for a vocation rather than for fun or to add to their general education." Other more recent studies, reported by Mayhew (15) support the earlier findings of the New York Regents and those included in Jacob's summary.

So far we have tried to outline some aspects of an effectively functioning person, and we have assumed that if a school curriculum were geared to developing such a person, its effects should at least be manifest in the values of its students. Next, we have pointed out that apparently the schools of today and yesterday are not and did not have an apparent effect in the area of students' values. What are some reasons that may explain this lack of relationship?

The conclusion that schools and schooling are not having much influence on the values of students is quite consistent with what social scientists have been observing and with what educators know about the teaching process as it is practiced in schools today. Sociologists and anthropologists have described in some detail the characteristics of the white collar American, the other directed person, and the organization man. Clearly these profiles do not depict the autonomous, reality perceiving, and competent person we have described as an effectively functioning individual. Evidently there are a great number of persons, products of the American schools, who have difficulty functioning effectively as we have defined it.

In addition, the evidence of teaching style dominant in the schools that has been reported by Hughes, Bellack, and Perkins seems to support Flanders' observation of the rule of 2/3's. This rule, an outgrowth of empirical analyses of teaching, suggests that teachers tend to play very direct roles in their classrooms. They do most of the talking and make most of the decisions. It would be difficult to argue that in such an environment, students could develop a sense of autonomy or the skills necessary for effective functioning.

Future Trends

The preceding paragraphs are not meant to imply that all is lost. The Yearbook Committee is able to perceive in the schools some notable counter-trends that augur well for the developing of effectively functioning students in the schools.

First, there seems to be a reaction against the notion that an educational experience can be summed up in an official statement of credit hours and grades. For instance, there was once an assumption that a bachelor's degree was equivalent to 128 hours of credit distributed in a fairly well-prescribed way. While such notions have been with us for several hundred years, they received a great deal of stature when concepts of efficiency borrowed from the business community began to play an important role in educational administration (5).

One outcome of this efficiency drive was the creation of the Carnegie Unit. If a course of English met for five hours a week, and if a student who completed such a course received a passing grade, then he was awarded one Carnegie Unit in English. While such units can easily be entered on transcripts and duly recorded in cumulative record folders, activities and learning experiences offered within the classroom are not actually evaluated or recorded. Recent innovations in general education at the collegiate level, such as the work at Sarah Lawrence College and Bennington and the flexible class scheduling of many secondary schools, have seemed to signal a significant attack upon this outmoded and limited view of education.

Second, there seems to be a growing awareness in the educational community of this nation that teachers do not have explicit objective standards that students must meet. More and more educators are beginning to realize that the judging role required of most teachers now is antithetical to the helping relationships so necessary in the developing of effectively functioning persons. Grading systems, regardless of their idiosyncrasies, are not amenable to comparison or, in most cases, even to use as descriptions of achievement. All grading systems, whether based on absolute percentages, estimates of growth, or on the normal curve make many important assumptions about learners and about learning that have little basis in fact. In sum, most teachers have difficulty expressing their standards in any operational way; have little rationale to defend the grading system they are using; and assess their students' work with measuring instruments that are at best of doubtful reliability and validity. The widening realization of this situation is causing a reappraisal of the teachers' role in the evaluation area. More and more schools are giving consideration to a sharp reduction in the judging role of the teacher. This trend may signal the approach of a new era in education—one that will serve better to promote the autonomy of our students in school and out of school.

Third, a shift in the emphasis of criticism of public schooling by persons both within and outside the profession seems to be coming. We seem to have passed the point of being disappointed in the lack of spelling ability, writing ability, and the lack of subject-matter skills on the part of many pupils. The critics of the schools are demanding these accomplishments and *more*. Schools are being asked to demonstrate their effectiveness in the areas of values, attitudes and thinking as well as in the areas of the three R's. Such a concern is also being reflected in the criticism that is becoming widespread of the standardized achievement tests, such as the New York State Regents examinations, that by and large test mainly recall and memory skills. More and more emphasis is being placed on the higher levels of cognitive skills—comprehension, analysis, application, synthesis and evaluation (4). This trend seems to indicate that a rather widespread consensus regarding education as the accumulation of facts is being replaced with a view that sees education as striving for profounder goals.

As a fourth point, it is becoming more and more respectable in our profession to be concerned with the cognitive aspects of children's development. After Professor Jerome Bruner addressed the ASCD national meeting in St. Louis several years ago, some people could be heard to say, "I wish he would concern himself with children." Such commentators seemed to hold the notion that if a teacher sets out to teach a child a concept or skill or fact he is demonstrating some basic lack of concern about the student's individuality. Such a view was generally accompanied by an implication that no information or skill is really worth teaching and that the main emphasis must be solely upon the teaching of process. The teaching of process, some maintain, is really to respect the individuality of students. A counter view that seems to reflect a current trend in curriculum planning is one that sees process as cognitive. It involves knowing. It is difficult to separate thinking as a process from the content. The commitment to teach "thinking" as a process carries with it the concomitant responsibility of dealing with the question, "Thinking about what?" This trend to see process and content as inseparable aspects of the curriculum is suggestive of curriculum opportunities that may develop more effectively functioning students.

Fifth, there is growing agreement among educators that the cognitive and affective domains cannot be neatly separated and dealt with at different times in the classroom. In the recent past, efforts to teach values or appreciations were scheduled as separate periods of courses in the curriculum. It was difficult, however, to find evidence of their effectiveness. More and more educators are coming to realize that all content has an affective dimension associated with it. Just as it is impossible to separate thinking as a process away from the object of thinking, so it is not possible to separate the valuing away from the knowledge of what is valued. Thus to prize, to appreciate, to revere implies a knowing. Newer analyses of teaching focusing on the cognitive and the affective domains may prove effective in promoting a curriculum that is more likely to produce autonomy, reasonable perceptions of reality, and competencies.

Finally, from the psychological constructs of "cognitive structure" there is new support for the view that facts and other bits of specific information have little or no meaning in and of themselves. It is only as facts are related to other ideas and to larger generalizations that the bits of information become meaningful. As students lose sight of the larger ideas to which the content is connected, the educational process becomes to them a rather sterile activity fraught with what Whitehead (19) termed "inert" ideas. For example, in many elementary schools, cloth is a unit of study in the second grade. Do we want our second graders to know about cloth, its sources, manufacture and uses? It seems more likely that a unit on cloth is designed to illumine and demonstrate some larger concept or generalization concerning man and his use of nature to meet his basic needs. Many times the generalizations that units such as the one on cloth are meant to illustrate are lost in the translation of the course of study guidebook into lesson plans.

When specifics of content are not seen by children as illustrative of some larger generalization, then children are dealing with Whitehead's "inert" ideas. Thus a welcome sign in curriculum planning is the trend in many of the new curriculum studies of stressing generalizations throughout the course of study. This trend can be seen in the newer curriculum studies in mathematics, biology and physics. Also, much of the current speculation in educational philosophy and curriculum is aimed at identifying and specifying the wider generalizations that make up the disciplines and at adapting them for inclusion in the curriculum plans of the schools (8). This approach may suggest the beginning of an era in education that is void of "inert" ideas that are so harmful to the educative process.

Implications for Teaching—The Evocative Environment

Some of the trends cited in the previous section are little more than glimmering sparks on the horizon of educational thought and practice while others are much brighter and more widely recognized. If these ideas do come into dominance in our schools in the next several decades, how will they be reflected in the teaching act? In keeping with our concerns for the child and the curriculum, two dimensions of the teaching process seem to be important aspects of what might be described as an evocative environment—a climate designed to produce feelings of autonomy, competency, and openness to experience. These dimensions concern themselves with the curriculum and the child.

The Curriculum

First, teachers' attitudes toward subject matter will change. They will feel that they are not teaching truth in any subject matter or discipline. Rather they will sense that they are teaching current explanations of reality—whether in science, history or English. They will attempt to communicate to their students the transcendent nature of what is being presented. Rival explanations will be explored or developed by the students. The history of each discipline will be searched for older explanations that were discarded for various reasons—and these reasons will be examined and will serve as a take-off point for discussions concerning the role of inquiry and new information in the history of thought.

In addition, teachers will sense that not all content is of equal importance. Some ideas are more relevant, more profound, more congruent with the concerns of students than are others. Teams of teachers and scholars from the disciplines will select important unifying generalizations from the disciplines and these will serve as the focus of the courses. The generalizations will not be presented as truths—but will be "discovered" in some cases or put to the test of reexamination and inquiry in others. Such teaching will reflect Whitehead's fifty year old recommendations for the mathematics curriculum which seem valid for all disciplines: select a few generalizations and teach them well **(19)**. Thus specifics presented in class—a single fact, a particular chemical reaction, or a unique event in history will be seen by students and teachers as examples or illustrations or counter-illustrations of an overarching generalization under consideration at that time.

Such a curriculum, focused on some of the important ideas of the disciplines and taught by teachers with a respect for doubt and new information, would provide for students an evocative environment found in few schools or universities today.

The Child

How will the trends identified earlier affect the teaching act *vis-à-vis* the child? The teacher will definitely be concerned with ideas *and* with children.

In working with an idea, a student on one hand may learn to say that it is true or valid. He may learn to say this on the same level as a parrot who learns to repeat certain statements. On the other hand, he may make it "his own" observation by reflecting upon the experiences he has had that have led him to this determination. Teachers who acknowledge this different level of learning will strive to encourage children to test, relate and reflect upon their formulations. To do this, the teacher must be skillful in setting up a climate that (a) encourages children to share their conceptions and preconceptions of reality and (b) allows children the opportunity to test their conceptions. A teacher who reflects the incipient trends identified in this chapter will stimulate the sharing of ideas and the testing of ideas by playing an *accepting, non-judging* role. As a teacher responds to children in a judging manner, he apparently takes away from students a feeling of freedom to express personal ideas and the opportunity to test ideas that they may have. To justify an idea with the phrase, "the teacher said so," is clearly falling back to the level of the parrot already cited.

In addition, in an aura of acceptance, the teacher may listen and accept almost any formulation a student may have about reality and then gently offer counter-examples. By providing dissonance of this sort, even when the formulations of the child agree with "the book," teachers will stimulate and motivate children to further inquiry and reflection into the matter under consideration. Teachers then will strive to help students reconstruct their curricular experiences by asking questions and by providing new opportunities leading to rival implications in a climate of acceptance. The teaching skills and strategies required for this sort of teaching have been suggested in earlier publications.[2] Such teaching is in sharp contrast to that described in the empirical studies of teaching reported by Flanders, Bellack and Hughes. In these descriptions of teaching, the categories that could be considered as mirroring acceptance and clarification of students' ideas on the part of teachers are almost always those containing the smallest frequencies. Indeed if there is a gap between what is preached in the colleges of education and what is practiced in the schools, it can be found in this area. There appear to be little clarification of ideas and a great deal of teacher-judgment expressed about students' ideas.

Summary

The question which this yearbook is focusing upon is essentially as follows: Are cognitive goals and concerns for children's effective functioning necessarily inconsistent? The Yearbook Committee's answer to this question is a loud and definite "no!" In an evocative environment, one which is accepting and challenging and one which views the disciplines as evolving tentative generalizations that may or may not stand the test of time, the values of both child and curriculum may be prized and preserved. It is our contention that such a point of view and such practice not only facilitate learning but provide an avenue for fostering mental health.

References

1. D. P. Ausubel. *The Psychology of Meaningful Verbal Learning*. New York: Grune and Stratton, 1963.
2. E. E. Bayles. *Democratic Educational Theory*. New York: Harper & Brothers, 1960.
3. A. A. Bellack. *The Language of the Classroom*. Report of Cooperative Research Project No. 1497. Washington, D.C.: U.S. Office of Education, 1963.
4. B. S. Bloom. *A Taxonomy of Educational Objectives: Cognitive Domain*. New York: McKay, 1956.
5. R. E. Callahan. *Education and the Cult of Efficiency*. Chicago: The University of Chicago Press, 1962.

[2] See Hunt and Metcalf (11); and Raths (17).

6. John Dewey. *The Child and the Curriculum.* Chicago: The University of Chicago Press, 1902.

7. Ned A. Flanders. *Teacher Influences, Pupil Attitudes and Achievement.* Report of Cooperative Research Project 397. Washington, D.C.: U.S. Office of Education, 1960.

8. G. W. Ford and Lawrence Pugno. *The Structure of Knowledge and the Curriculum.* Chicago: Rand McNally and Company, 1964.

9. Ronald Gross. "Two-Year-Olds Are Very Smart." *New York Times Magazine.* September 6, 1964. p. 10-11.

10. M. M. Hughes. *Development of the Means for the Assessment of the Quality of Teaching in the Elementary Schools.* Report of Cooperative Research Project No. 353. Washington, D.C.: U.S. Office of Education, 1960.

11. M. P. Hunt and L. E. Metcalf. *Teaching High School Social Studies.* New York: Harper & Brothers, 1955.

12. P. E. Jacob. *Changing Values in College.* New York: Harper & Brothers, 1957.

13. M. Jahoda. *Current Concepts of Positive Mental Health.* New York: Basic Books, Inc., 1958.

14. L. S. Kubie. "Research in Protecting Preconscious Functions in Education." *Nurturing Individual Potential.* Washington, D.C.: Association for Supervision and Curriculum Development, 1961. p. 28-42.

15. Lewis B. Mayhew. *General Education: An Account and Appraisal.* New York: Harper & Brothers, 1960.

16. H. V. Perkins. "A Procedure for Assessing the Classroom Behavior." *American Educational Research Journal I* 4:249-59; November 1964.

17. James Raths. "A Strategy for Developing Values." *Educational Leadership* 21: 509-14, 554; May 1964.

18. Frank T. Spaulding. *High School and Life: The Regents Inquiry.* New York: McGraw-Hill Book Co., 1938.

19. A. N. Whitehead. *The Aims of Education.* New York: The Macmillan Company, 1929.

The Achievement of Competency

To function competently as a human being one needs to be able to work, to play and to love. One acquires the skills, knowledge and feelings to do these things in the humanizing or key integrative institutions of our culture. The primary prerequisite for human competency is to learn to use symbols to differentiate, identify and hold onto objects and events, to perceive objects and events accurately, to manage healthfully heavy emotional loads or periods of little or no environmental stress, to increase the nature and kind of metaphors by which self, others and the world are perceived and conceived, and to take in all these symbols in an integrative and connected fashion.

The processes of education are teacher-content-pupil interactions which lead to the development of these skills inherent in effective ego processes. The development of such skills is the joint concern of educational and community mental health programs.

2

The Achievement of Competency

Eli M. Bower

TO BE competent in the world of tomorrow one needs to be able to do three things—to love, to work and to play. To define these competencies operationally requires the courage of a lion tamer and the linguistic ability of a modern Shakespeare. Nevertheless, to live in and with a group or society one needs to feel himself part of others and to have sufficient self to be able to give some of this to others (love); to be able to contribute one's skill and energies to the general welfare and receive reimbursement in hard cash or a reasonable facsimile (work); and to find enjoyable avenues of activity to escape the real world (play). The aim of this chapter is to pursue and hopefully overtake those educational processes which seem to be most promising in helping students learn to become competent human beings—human beings who can love, work and play effectively.

Basically the business of a society and its institutions is to produce competent adults out of growing, immature (i.e., incompetent) children. We have therefore in our despair and wisdom created and preserved humanizing institutions—institutions whose major purpose is to induct children into the goals and values of a society, the rules by which the significant "games" are played and the skills and learnings required to play the games well. These humanizing institutions I choose to call "primary" since they attempt to provide a safe and effective passage between birth and adulthood for all members of our society. Such societal arrangements as the family, health agencies, school, child care centers and recreation departments are primarily constructed to help children as they grow up and, at the same time, to help parents survive the process. As any fortunate parent or interested participant can testify, the flowering of a child into a mature, competent adult is indeed the most satisfying show on earth; however, such growth cannot proceed without nurture by the institutions which society has designated for this function.

Our concern here is with the school's role as a primary institution, its ability to influence other primary institutions and its openness to change by the other agencies, especially the economic and political institutions. School does not start for children until they have had extensive experiences in other institutions such as home, play and health agencies. A child's experience in these agencies can give him quite a lead or handicap as he enters school. One of the prime purposes of the family is to provide the child with sufficient affective nutrient and home base support so that, as he grows, he feels safe enough to risk exploring the real and symbolic world around him. The health agencies provide basic biological, developmental and—where necessary—medical guidance to produce the physical and mental robustness required to take the normal risks of life. The play agencies (including informal play groups) provide the group experiences prerequisite to the use of symbols.

With these three "givens," home, health and play experience, education can proceed at a merry and productive pace. With minor or major lacks in these preschool experiences, children may find themselves searching for major makeup courses for these deficiencies before going on to other matters. Often such makeup courses are not available in the school since these prerequisites are assumed to have been obtained by all children before school entrance.

To function effectively in school, children need both cognitive and emotional abilities. In all human matters these two functions are inseparably locked together. For discussion purposes let us separate the emotional or mental health aspects of education and examine first the emotional or mental health concept in relation to human competency.

Mental Health and Mental Health Processes

The concept of mental health was born out of the problems of mental illness midwifed by Clifford W. Beers and the Connecticut Society for Mental Hygiene. Mr. Beers, who had just recovered from both a mental illness and a harrowing experience in a mental institution, gathered a group of interested citizens together in New Haven in 1908 to form the above-mentioned society, which was pledged to work for the conservation of mental health and to help prevent nervous and mental disorders. The following year, Beers helped to create the National Committee for Mental Hygiene which has grown up to become the National Association for Mental Health (18).

The behavior of non-sick human beings toward those with mental and emotional disorders has, in the past, shaken the minds of sensitive historians. In the 15th century approximately 100,000 persons (a conservative estimate) were burned at the stake for having daydreams or hallucinations or being the object of someone else's daydreams or hallucinations. The records of witch trials contain what today would be a solid clinical testimony to the fact that many of the persons burned and mutilated were afflicted with schizophrenia or schizophrenic states; the emotional health of the witch finders, keepers and burners was, in the light of present knowledge, probably even worse. Until well into the middle of the 19th century, most mentally ill patients were kept chained and closeted in asylums. In 1792 Philippe Pinel, a Parisian physician appointed as superintendent of the hospital at Salpetriére, proposed unchaining the "beasts" and substituting treatment for terror. This notion gained as much support as a Republican candidate at a Democratic convention; it took another hundred years for society to begin to move toward this notion.

Major changes in care and treatment awaited a better understanding of the causes and meaning of mental illness. This did not come until Freud, his followers, modifiers and dissenters made available theories of biological and personality development which could be used in conceptualizing mental illnesses and planning treatment interventions.

. In 1955 the U.S. Congress authorized the establishment of a nongovernmental, multidisciplinary, nonprofit organization—The Joint Commission on Mental Illness and Health and asked this body to conduct a study of mental health and illness in the U.S. The first aspect of the study was undertaken by Marie Jahoda on the nature of positive mental health (14). The book emphasized that mental health is only one of many human goals and is not an ultimate goal in itself—it is a means to an end and not the end itself. Mental health as a concept has been a vague and confused idea and has aroused some perplexity among clinical and behavioral scientists as an object of study or definition because of this. In addition, the casting onto the state of "mental health" the virtues of composed and exemplary behavior has also helped to move it in the direction of the scientific doghouse.

In general, concepts of mental health have included the ability to adapt to one's environment, ability to perceive reality accurately, the ability to manage stress healthfully, the ability to stand on one's own two feet, the ability to learn and a feeling of well being. All of these are moderate to high level abstractions and difficult to translate into operational terms. One can, as Jahoda does, tie these abilities up with adequacy in love, work, play and interpersonal relations.

What does mental health mean to the child in school, his teachers, principal and parents? When one proposes to promote mental health through educational processes, how exactly does one do this (3)? The heart of the answer is that the enhancement of mental health in children is not a separate activity of the school but develops as part of the social and individual transactions between the child and his school environment. One does not take a course in mental health to become mentally healthier. Educational and mental health processes are like the wool skein in a sweater, inextricably interwoven. However, unlike the Emperor's new clothes, this sweater must provide for the wearer real knowledge, skills and intellectual content.

The Processes of Education

There are as many assumptions about education and educational processes as there are about human nature and human behavior. Before launching into the more theoretical and the more specific program aspects of education and competency, it would be well to clarify several postulates upon which the rest of the chapter is based. These are:

1. The school has become a major primary or key integrative agency for children. All children need to undergo successfully the expressive, social and content demands of the school. One cannot skip blithely through this system with a kind face and a bland smile and emerge "educated."

2. Learning "school" skills is the basic business of children in school. A child who fails to learn these skills "has given hostages to fortune." His ability to function as a child and as an adult is increasingly limited.

3. Schools are transmitters and generators of symbolic lore and symbolic skills. The essence of education is learning to use symbols effectively as representation of objects, events and relationships in creative and interpersonal activities.

4. Education is a cognitive-affective mediation [1] of content by a student. The mediation or processing of the content is done by that part of the personality called ego processes.

---

[1] Mediation is used here to mean an active managing and interpreting of information.

5. To be educationally successful, students must learn to develop competent and effective mediational or ego processes.

6. Information which is not mediated or acted on by ego processes becomes a kind of intellectual shellac which often serves to give a high gloss to an empty house.

7. The process of learning involves the development and utilization of five distinctive but overlapping ego processes. These are:

a. The processes of experiencing a wide variety of objects (including self), events and feelings and attaching symbols to them (differentiation)

b. The processes of binding objects, events and feelings with accurate symbols in a firm but not untieable knot (fidelity)

c. The processes of managing heavy or light cognitive-affective loads via regulation of informational inputs and the discharge of stress (pacing)

d. The processes of taking on new metaphors and matrices or revising old metaphors and matrices in perceiving oneself and the world (expansion)

e. The processes of assimilating new information and integrating it within appropriate layers of the personality (integration).

8. Meaningful learning involves a student, learning content and a mediator-teacher. For students, all learning is undergone in personality matrices which not only give direction to the meaning of the content to the learner but determine its eventual use. Knowing is a conglomerate of cognitive-emotional symbols which get attached to experiences but stay on in ego processes.

Intelligence and Emotion

The concept of intelligence as the ability to learn usually brooks no argument. One prevailing concept of intelligence is that it is an attribute a person has much of, little of, or a normal amount of. Intelligence is therefore believed to be measurable and it is often recorded as a somewhat variable but fixed quantity. Emotion, on the other hand, is "felt" and is therefore a hazy mist from the Land of Oz. Emotion itself is often associated only with demonstrable feelings. But is someone with strong emotions weak? On what dimensions do we tackle this vague yet critical notion? How is emotion quantified? Is more emotion better than less? Is being emotional preferable to not being so? High intelligence can be appreciated and used. How does one appreciate and use "high" or optimal emotion?

It is important at this point to differentiate the concept of intellect from that of intelligence, since, as Hofstadter points out and documents, our society prizes intelligence but is somewhat dubious or ambivalent about intellect. The manifest difference seems to be epitomized by the frequent use of intellectual as an epithet. The significant distinction seems to be that intelligence as a concept has latched onto meanings associated with the doing, the immediate, the useful and the practical. Intellect, on the other hand, "examines, ponders, wonders, theorizes, criticizes, imagines . . . evaluates evaluations and looks for the meanings of situations as a whole" (11).

Emotion is energy activated by symbols. Yet symbols are the prime vehicles for intelligent or intellectual behavior. The intellectual power of such symbols depends on how they are bound into the experiences and the personality apparatus of the child. One might, for example, consider the clarity and logic of the thought processes of a paranoid individual which often lead him to the inevitable and sensible (to him) conclusion that violence is necessary for self protection. Or one might look at an early study by Wechsler (21) who attempted to identify the total amount of intellective factors which could be accounted for in tests of intelligence and found that it seldom exceeded 60 percent of the total factors. On the basis of this and other studies, Wechsler concluded that general intelligence or IQ could not be equated with intellectual ability alone but must be regarded as a manifestation of the personality as a whole.

However we may talk or write about intellect and emotion as independent dimensions of functioning, they are highly interdigitated and reinforcing functions. This relationship is illustrated in a 14-year-old boy with an above average IQ who failed an item on the Stanford-Binet Intelligence Test which asks the subject to explain the commonality of concepts. In explaining what tall and short have in common the boy said, "If a short boy walks with a tall girl and doesn't mind it, it makes no difference." In explaining what heavy and light have in common he replied, "If a task is heavy and you don't mind doing it, then it is light" (15). One does not need to be a psychologist to conclude that the boy's emotional biases were reducing his powers of cognitive discrimination and freedom.

If one were to try to put emotion and intellect together into some useful metaphor, the concept of "degrees of freedom" or enhancing of action alternatives is most useful. Educational and socialization experiences can be regarded as processes intended to increase the functioning possibilities of human behavior. To accomplish this the individual must be able to take in and assimilate information, data, knowledge and other environmental inputs so that the individual is better able to take in and assimilate additional information. If this seems circular, it is. The object of learning or living is to make further learning and living more possible.

Emotional constrictions and defects limit perceptions and environmental inputs as well as close down avenues for feedback. Where education and feeling are separated and fragmented and there is no bridge between them, intellectual storing may go on with little or no effect on behavior or personality growth. On the other hand, emotional development rarely takes place without well played emotional and cognitive "matches" between the child and his environment. Emotional support or love, in its pure sense, could not by itself produce the happy, productive child unless such support or love were hinged onto the learning of significant cognitive or developmental tasks. A healthy emotional relationship between a child and a parent would supply the basic harmony and orchestration to the main theme of development which involves a child learning competence in and about his environment.

The concept of "degrees of freedom" can best be conceptualized with the help of a metaphor proposed by a former President of the United States:

We say of a boat skimming the water with light foot, "How free she runs," when we mean how perfectly she is adjusted to the force of the wind, how perfectly she obeys the great breath out of the heaven that fills her sails. Throw her head up into the wind and see how she will halt and stagger, how every sheet will shiver and her whole frame be shaken, how instantly she is "in irons" in the expressive phrase of the sea. She is free only when you have let her fall off again and have recovered once more her nice adjustment to the forces she must obey and cannot defy (24).

The competence of a sailboat may be regarded as a function of its ability to deal with its environment—the water, the wind and its own structure. A race among sailboats of the same class places key responsibility for enhancing the competence of each craft on the crew and especially on the skipper. The integration of sail, weight, wind and rigging will send the craft speeding along in its characteristic picturesque manner. A lack of integration or coordination may slow her down or capsize her.

As someone once said, ships are safe in a harbor but then what are ships for? Children find their initial anchor in the home but their destination is to move out into society and contribute what they can to themselves and others. The development of the skills of emotional competence are part of the skills of learning to eat, walk, talk, read and think. To be mentally healthy one must attain competence in knowing as well as feeling. To paraphrase Samuel Johnson, "Healthy emotions without knowledge are weak and useless and knowledge without healthy emotions is dangerous and dreadful."

All individuals find themselves somewhat "in irons" as a result of early emotional experiences. However, such slight degrees of emotional restriction do not seriously impair functioning. The mainspring of emotional controls may be below awareness—in past events, feelings and experiences which are not readily available to intellectual scrutiny by the individual himself. The crux of the problem is that the energy so stored seeks outlets and goals which are difficult to attain since they can only be reached by replaying childish games and capturing symbolic goals. As a result, emotional energy stored below levels of awareness tend to restrict behavioral alternatives and reduce behavior to automatic, repetitive and inflexible patterns of response.

Emotional-intellectual distress such as mental disorders or illnesses may restrict the individual to one or two possible responses. This inflexibility in a world made up of myriads of flitting and shifting transactions is bound to result in interpersonal friction or intrapersonal distress. The essence of the difference between the emotionally free individual and the markedly restricted one is, as Kubie puts it, the degree of hardening of behavior into patterns of comparative unalterability. In the highly neurotic or psychotic individual the patterns of behavior are virtually frozen.

An Early Marriage of Emotion and Intellect and Its Offspring

Once upon a time intellect and emotion were married and gave birth to a basic instructional and learning principle called the Law of Effect. The marriage had been in the offing for many years since each had agreed one could not live without the other. The progeny was a well rounded generalization which stated that the association of cognitive or intellective learnings with "pleasurable" feelings leads to successful and rapid learning; conversely, learnings which arrive simultaneously with unpleasure, pain or annoyance lead to non-assimilation and nonlearning. This principle, often called CC (Contiguous Conditioning) or RC (Reinforcement Conditioning), grew into a well developed and vigorous organism.

One of the puzzling facts about this law was that apparently some children who were repeatedly punished for errors seldom learned to correct their responses. Some even did worse. Studies (Sears, Maccoby and Levin) (19) of children with high degrees of dependency also seemed to behave counter to such laws. For example, mothers who behaved toward young, dependent children in a punishing manner, i.e., by scolding, impatience or irritation, tended to increase the child's dependency. On the other hand, dependence was often decreased by a mother's rewarding the child's dependency or clinging demands.

To further complicate the picture, the influence of punishment was found most devastating on children who had had the most pleasant experiences in resolving dependency needs. What the Law of Effect may have overlooked is the organizing processes of the individual in response to environmental stimuli. For example, the impact of punishment on a child is a function of his notion of its meaning. If the punishment is perceived to be inconsistent and confusing with past experiences, the response of the organism may often be highly upsetting and vigorous.

Somewhere between the source of environmental stimuli and organismic responses is a dark tunnel or black box which reaches out in both directions and patterns all incoming vehicles so that the tunnel and the organism are both changed. This dark tunnel has been conceptualized as ego or, more correctly, ego processes. The nub of competency lies in the effectiveness of these personality processes.

The Essence of Ego Processes

An illustrative experiment by Humphreys (13), one of a number of similar experiments, amplifies the basic organizing aspect of ego processes. In the experiment, subjects are seated in front of a board with two bulbs which light up together or one at a time. The experimental task is to predict whether or not when left light is lit, right will follow. Two different kinds of experiences were given to subjects. Group one got "right light always follows left;" group two, "right light follows left in about half the cases" (the half-lit group). As one would predict, the first group learned to predict right would follow left faster than the second group learned to predict right followed left only half the time.

After a brief interval both groups were given a new pattern—left light but no following red light. Now on the basis of the reinforcement or conditioning theory of learning, one would surmise that the original "half-lit" group two would learn this new pattern faster than group one since they had had less reinforcement and less conditioning to the first learning exercise. Group one, of necessity, would have to unlearn more and loosen more reinforcements than group two. However, as one might guess, group one learned the new pattern faster and was able to shift response gears more readily. The inference which is most probably correct is that what is learned in any experience, including a simple experimental one like this, is organized and patterned by the learner through his ego processes. The pattern of stimuli given to group one was regular and consistent and therefore easily organized as a concept or pattern. Group two had to work harder to find the organizational glue and as a result the pattern took on less clarity and sharpness. When the pattern was changed, the subjects with the tighter concept were quickly aware that something different was going on. The group with the loosely organized pattern apparently learned this more slowly.

The somewhat overblown, yet relevant implication of this experiment suggests the primacy of the organizing qualities of the person in learning. Another example of this organizing quality of ego processes is given by Vernon (20) in his experiences with subjects who lived for a period of time in a lightproof and soundproof room in the basement of Princeton's Eno Hall. This type of sensory deprivation environment is the epitome of a boring and monotonous existence. Most subjects have to be paid to live in it and are quite happy to get out as soon as possible. Vernon reported one subject who enjoyed his experience and who upon release requested additional confinement. The puzzled experimenters questioned the subject who at first said all he wanted was food and rest and offered to do additional time free of charge. Finally, it came out that the subject, a national of a Middle Eastern country who was studying politics in the U.S., anticipated that upon his return to his country he would end up a political prisoner in solitary confinement. Thus he conceptualized the experiment as a rehearsal for the real thing and spent his time "practicing," to him a very significant and meaningful experience. It was "enjoyable" in the sense that mastery of a future difficult task could be accomplished in this simulated or play environment.

Ego processes like electricity cannot be seen or denoted; they can only be described through inference but as in electricity the impact of such inferences can be felt and seen. Descriptively, ego processes can be defined as that part of the personality of an individual which selects, mediates and symbolically binds inputs from the external or internal environments. Ego processes do all this to protect and enhance the organism. Such processes are basically survival processes although often the price paid seems hardly a fair exchange.

The essence of ego processing lies in its mediation and binding of objects, events and feelings. Mediation of inputs implies active participation by the organism in defining the perception and working out the best response from all available alternatives. As has been mentioned, ego processes have sometimes been conceptualized as taking place in a black box or tunnel through which stimuli pass to become responses. Since the terrain of the tunnel is unobservable, behavioral cartographers have had to infer its topography and substructural terrain. Some of these courageous geographers have located in this Stygian darkness, motives, instincts, faculties, contiguities, effects, dissonance, reinforcement and other twisting hills and valleys. Others distressed by the lack of light and clear vision in the tunnel abolished it. Still others behave like the man who decides to search for a lost article under a lit lamppost where he can see rather than in the darkness where the article was lost. Or one can study stimulus response mechanisms in lower animals with the hope that shedding light here will provide clues to the human tunnel.

Mediation activities on the part of ego processes include an active scanning and selecting of inputs. All inputs are polarized by ego processes, i.e., they can be *differentiated,* reproduced with good *fidelity, paced, expanded* and *integrated* on the one hand or *diffused, distorted, overloaded, constricted* or *fragmented* on the other. These dimensions will be discussed further in the following section. In any case, ego processes put their own twist on the input ball which at times may emerge as a sharp curve, wild pitch, or cannonball.

The process of mediation not only modifies and changes inputs but is alert to the organism's response to inputs. Such responses also become inputs to the extent to which ego processes allow and encourage such feedback. Modifications and changes of stimuli and responses are performed through symbols which are the vehicles which pass back and forth through the tunnel. In part, the change is a result of the bindings or loads on each symbol which are incorporated into ego processes. It is as if small armies marching through the tunnel left numbers of their men stationed at significant posts before leaving the scene. These symbolic soldiers stand guard in the tunnel ready to capture and bind other vehicles. The crux of the problem of human competency, i.e., the ability to love, work and play, is a manifestation of the mediation and binding processes of the ego.

Conflict and Conflict-free Ego Processes

The notion of ego processes if not actually conceived by the Freuds (father and daughter) was certainly brought into the educational and psychological awareness by them. In S. Freud's theory, ego processes were derived from basic biological or sexual energy or drives (id) as a mechanism of coping with the conflicts between inner drives and the outer environment. The ego, said Freud, has the task of self preservation:

As regards external events, it performs that task by becoming aware of the stimuli from without, by storing up experiences of them (in the memory), by avoiding excessive stimuli (through flight), by dealing with modern stimuli (through adaptation) and finally by learning to bring about appropriate modifications in the external events in relation to the id, it performs that task by gaining control over the demands of the instincts by deciding whether they shall be allowed to obtain satisfaction by postponing that satisfaction to times and circumstances favorable in the external world or by suppressing their excitations completely. . . . Thus an action by the ego is as it should be if it satisfies simultaneously the demands of the id, of the superego (precipitate in the ego of parental influence), of reality, that is to say if it is able to reconcile their demands with one another.[2]

Hartmann, Buhler and others in the 1930's and '40's began to examine the notion that some areas of ego functioning might be considered "conflict-free." By this they meant that ego processes found pleasure and strength in activities on their own, in doing something well, in solving a problem for its own sake, in dancing, conversing or walking in the woods. In other words, in addition to ego processes arising from and being developed out of broad sexual drives or energies, such processes may emerge and grow from the organism's effectiveness and enjoyment of the environment and self. Such perhaps is a young child in a kitchen experiencing pots, pans and ladles. Or a group of children jumping, running and skipping for the fun of it.

Play has been found to be a major activity in ego development. Why is play participated in often passionately and at times with frenzy and absorptive seriousness? Or where is the fun in watching play—what do millions of Americans get out of a football or basketball game? Since each spectator is paying for it voluntarily in money and time, where is its payoff?

Play is different from ordinary living, yet it is often difficult to differentiate when play ends and non-play begins. Theatergoers emerge grim and angry at Albee's drama, *Who's Afraid of Virginia Woolf?*, in part because of the difficulty one has in separating games from reality in the "play." We often use the expression "what's his game?"—meaning what are his goals and by what rules is he behaving? However one differentiates play from non-play in children's behavior, play is a voluntary activity. An order to play, for children, cannot be play. As a voluntary activity, play permits a stepping out of life or a moratorium in living, so to speak, to rehearse physical and mental tasks which are deemed important and significant to the individual. All play takes place within specified or implied rules which are absolutely binding. Chessmen can only be moved as prescribed. Tag is it. In playing house, mothers cook and fathers read the paper. The rules of the game cannot be broken without penalty, so laws cannot be broken without (if caught) punishment. To be able to play—to cast off life and enjoy a playful temporary existence—is one of the outcomes of effective ego processes. This will be discussed further at the end of this chapter.

[2] Sigmund Freud. *An Outline of Psychoanalysis*. New York: W. W. Norton & Co., 1949. p. 15. This page and the following provide an excellent description and definition of ego processes.

Implications of Autonomous Ego Processes

The resurgence in interest in ego processes, especially the conflict-free aspects, has led to some changes in the direction of mental health, social welfare and education programs. Although it would not be fair to say that such changes are marked and clear, the trend of new federal programs, such as the Peace Corps, Job Corps, the Economic Opportunity Act, Operation Head Start, Community Mental Health Programs and related changes in mental health programs in the States points in a new direction.

This shift is away from an intrapsychic model of human effectiveness to a social competency one. The basic differences, given in Table I, highlight the extremes of these models. Such differences are not discrete or exclusive. In practice, persons concerned with relief of intrapsychic distress are also concerned with social competence and vice versa.

Table I: Contrasts in the Social Competency and Intrapsychic Models of Mental Health

Social Competency Model	Intrapsychic Model
1. Aim is functioning effectiveness—anxiety relevant only to extent to which it reduces and interferes with or stimulates and enhances this goal.	1. Aim is intrapsychic comfort—"peace of mind." Surplus anxiety seen as major block to this goal.
2. Goal is to learn how to carry on those transactions with environment which assist the individual in gaining individual and social competence.	2. Goal is mental health—emotional freedom to act, think and feel with increasing levels of awareness.
3. Goals measured by increased fitness or ability in functioning.	3. Goals measured by clinical or subjective judgment.
4. Program leverage is primarily task centered—objective is learning new skills including behavioral skills.	4. Program leverage is primarily affective and focused on self understanding.
5. Conceptually allied to "conflict-free" spheres of ego processes.	5. Conceptually allied to conflicts in ego-id-superego relations.
6. Approach is primarily a direct, mediative one—ego building.	6. Approach is primarily an indirect, unmediative one—peeling away of obsolescent ego defenses.
7. Focus is on increasing competency in present developmental tasks.	7. Focus is on intrapsychic blocks to functioning—freeing individual to act or think.
8. Based on achieving conscious satisfactions—pleasure felt in neuromuscular system.	8. Based on achieving internal symbolic satisfactions—finding suitable outlets for feelings and drives.
9. Individual study leads to environmental and social system manipulation.	9. Individual study leads to individual "therapy."
10. Conceptualizes a continuum of social incompetencies due to emotional problems ranging from mild to severe.	10. Conceptualizes a dichotomy between those who are sick and those who are not.

Competence as a Function of Ego Processes of Differentiation

One of the most basic and early processes in ego development is the separation of self from the environment and its delineation as a conceptual springboard for perceptions and behavior. To a great extent the development of this ego dimension is a function of early emotional nutrition from parents and an environment which provides an opportunity for a variety of active and creative experiences with objects, events and persons. Early social and environmental deprivation produce ego processes which perceive objects and events diffusely; metaphorically one could say the poor resolving power of the ego makes objects, events and persons appear out of focus and difficult to recognize. What is "figure" may appear to be "ground"; what is "ground" may look like "figure." Or they may blend imperceptibly in specific areas of overlap. As Bruner points out: "Not only does early deprivation rob the organism of the opportunity of constructing models of the environment, it also prevents the development of efficient strategies for evaluating information—for finding out what leads to what and with what likelihood" (4).

The ego processes of diffusion lead to inadequate differentiation of the environment and inadequate attachments between symbols and objects, events and relationships. Ego processes which have low differentiating abilities have difficulty binding cognitive-affective information effectively. Such deficiencies are often the result of a lack by children of representational symbols by which objects can be named, events mediated into experiences and individuals related to as persons. The result is a lack of symbolic tools and skills from which the sparking between the human being and his environment can proceed and develop.

Where there are marked degrees of deprivation of sensory experiences because of a child's environment or constitution, the results can be devastating on the organism. Kubzansky and Leiderman (16) in an overview of research on sensory deprivation cite research studies which show that such deprivation in the early life of the child creates *permanent* living difficulties and that without adequate environmental stimulation the cognitive-affective growth of the individual is deficient and atypical. Examination of studies of maternal deprivation also reveals that at least part of this deprivation is a severe reduction in variety and amount of sensory stimulation (9).

In addition the work of a number of investigators, leaning on the work of Hebb, has confirmed the notion that varied environmental stimulation is a necessary factor in human development and is probably a result of what Hebb called "the immediate drive value of cognitive experience" (10). Thus ego processes of differentiation are necessary to push the organism into exploratory or manipulative experiences in an attempt to master the complex environment and become competent in it. And conversely early exploratory or manipulative experiences can help produce those ego processes which can process and bind such learning for future use.

The lack of effective differentiating ego processes in large segments of our child population provides one of the major challenges to public education. How does one teach reading to a child unable to find a "hook" in his environmental experience on which to hang a word, a sentence or paragraph? Or how does a lower class Negro child conceptualize a book or television program showing a father returning from work, playing ball with him in the backyard, and sitting down to a family dinner, complete with conversation and dessert?

Large cities like New York have had to contend with vast in-migration of populations whose cultural and language experiences limited their ego differentiating processes. As of October 31, 1961, the New York City School Board estimated 225,000 of the 573,000 elementary school children and 75,000 of the 186,000 junior high school students to be disadvantaged in learning to learn in school. The initiation of a program called Higher Horizons, begun in September 1959, was based on the principle of compensatory education and differential use of services to raise levels of aspiration and educational competency in specific groups of children. Much of the effort of the Higher Horizons program has gone into increasing the degrees of freedom of teachers to function with disadvantaged children. In addition the program aimed at increasing the scope of the child's environment through trips to art museums, ballets, operas, puppet shows, concerts, libraries, parks and banks, special instructional programs, counseling students and parents, group guidance and a great deal of activity with parents and the community. Other programs of this kind are now under way in other communities.

Competence as a Function of Ego Processes of Fidelity

The specific nature of events, of objects and of relationships must be differentiated and separated one from another. In addition they must be assimilated and symbolized by the ego processes with clarity and accuracy. One can learn to separate one's self from the environment and from others; the fidelity dimension is concerned with the accuracy of such separation and the conciseness of symbolic attachments related to these processes.

All sensory inputs are distorted since all ego processes are products of socializing experiences which are idiosyncratic and personal in their impact. All perceptions are deviations from or approximations of the external fact if one could agree on the existence of an external fact without a viewer.

Ego processes which have high fidelity mediate inputs in a consensually validated manner. On the other hand, ego processes which distort inputs do so out of the defensive needs of the organism. These distorting mechanisms carry such tags as projection (the casting onto others of one's own feelings or attitudes), reaction formation (taking on behavior which is directly opposite to inner feelings), undoing (repeating the sequence of an activity in an effort to replace the original act or event) and displacement (transference of feelings from one relationship to another)—to name a few. Ego processes which distort objects, events or relationships cannot be corrected easily. Often such distortion is a result of unconscious processes which operate below the level of awareness of the individual.

The child who has marked tendencies to distort often needs individual help from mental health agencies. The school's job is the enhancement and promotion of learning experiences in which symbols are correctly related to their environmental referents. In fact education can be considered the process of mediating symbols so that they are bound firmly (but not too firmly) and accurately within the ego processes of the individual.

The teacher's job in essence is to help the child learn and incorporate the denotative and connotative meanings of symbols avoiding the flat, binary Aristotelian dichotomies which tend to arise in the process. Moreover the school must provide for many children the real objects, events and relationships to which symbols can be tied accurately. To talk about democracy, for example, may be a meaningless abstraction unless this abstraction is given roots and binding in a meaningful event. Unless this is done, such words are like boats in a storm—tossed this way or that depending on the level of abstraction of the symbol. Learning firmly anchored in real, i.e., experienced, events is less likely to be distorted.

Competence as a Function of Ego Processes of Pacing

The end product of socialization and educational experience is an individual's ability to control and regulate his aggressive and impulsive drives. This means ego processes must develop the ability to process large gulps of emotion as in periods of crisis as well as to deal with periods of ennui and boredom. Pacing is the ability to take the slings and arrows of misfortune without the need to blow up or cave in, and in dull or depressed periods to develop and hold onto sufficient inner feelings to remain interested and concerned with the problems of living.

Ego processes which cannot pace inputs become overloaded. An object, event or relationship which becomes emotionally overloaded can weigh down its symbol so that the symbol becomes highly charged like a Leyden jar. As a result, the symbol as stored in the ego processes is tightly bound to an object or event and when discharged, can cause quite an explosion. Or in other cases, the overloading can result in a shying away from any possible new stimuli so that the individual tends to live in a bland and sterile manner avoiding events and relationships which may drain or pain his emotional boils.

Two types of school experiences may be helpful to a child in developing pacing competency. One is the conscious and planned introduction of humor into the basic school curriculum. One has but to glance through *101 Elephant Jokes* as compiled by Bob Blake, age 14, and published by Scholastic Magazines (2), to recognize the need children have to play with words and untie some of the bindings on those cultural vehicles which may be too restrictive. For example: "How do you stop a herd of elephants from charging?" "Take away their credit cards!" is a form of word play which allows "charging" to change context rather abruptly and surprisingly. There is a loosening of the binding of words and concepts which encourages the development of spontaneity and logic in children and which often is lost in adolescence and adulthood.

To be able to use humor suggests that the ego processes of a student can, to some degree, differentiate between seriousness and play. William Fry, Jr., states:

> Participation in play and humor provides opportunity for practice with this balancing skill. Becoming skilled in playing or joking (or riddle telling or slapstick) provides one with a degree of skill in maintaining one's equilibrium of the two antithetical states—spontaneity and thoughtfulness. When balance is stable, the spontaneity of the ongoing process of life is not paralyzed by the detachment of thoughtfulness of self watchfulness or is not lost in a hysteria of spontaneity (7).

Moreover a child's delight in play could be extended into the arena of mass groans—the pun. Punning does have the virtue of constantly reminding all those in hearing distance of the arbitrary nature of symbols. When we shift the context of "charge" from elephant to credit card, we have been pleasantly tricked and refreshed. As Boswell puts it, "A good pun may be admitted among the smaller excellencies of lively conversation."

A second curriculum resource to develop pacing and to avoid overloading has to do with the use of puppets or other devices for role playing. The use of appropriate problem stories or short dramatic sketches can make excellent unloading platforms. Teachers of English, social studies, history, drama, languages or other curricula in which the drama and crisis of life can be felt and played out have unequaled opportunity to make such experiences available as part of the regular curriculum. In literature students can be touched by the individual or interpersonal problems of others. A skillful teacher can help students identify and express these cognitive-affective responses with understanding and insight.

Competence as a Function of the Ego Processes of Expansion

Education is the business of expanding ego processes by developing new concepts and metaphors by which information can be assimilated and arranged. In addition ego processes facing a variety of normal crises and stress seek to learn to manage these successfully. As a consequence of such successful management, the individual is better equipped conceptually to handle other stresses.

The antithesis of expansion is constriction. Constricted ego processes limit the amount and kind of information and new conceptual inputs which can be taken in and which as a result limit growth and change. As a result such processes hold an individual to a prescribed number of alternatives or choices in responding to the environment. Symbols are used rigidly and spontaneity is severely curtailed. Channels to and from the environment have hardened and in doing so have frozen the person in place.

Where expansion is possible (where constriction is not the result of major unconscious factors in the personality) the doors and gateways are the meaningful conceptual themes of history, science, mathematics, economics, English, literature and even psychology. The ego boundary between self and the world is semipermeable; the osmotic process of change is the meaningful concept or metaphor.

Education, as its Latin etymology indicates, is primarily an ego expansion process—a leading or drawing out. As new concepts are assimilated in the self, ego processes expand toward new concepts of self, others and the world. One of the royal roads to ego expansion is reading competence—a combination of reading enjoyment and reading skill. Reading maketh the full man, as Bacon noted. It is one of the few magic vehicles by which new possibilities, new ideas, new visions can be born to man—no matter what his lot in life. As Richard Wright states so incisively in his biography:

It had been my accidental reading of fiction and literary criticism that had evoked in me vague glimpses of life's possibilities . . . and it was out of these novels, stories and articles, out of the emotional impact of imaginative constructions of heroic or tragic deeds that I felt touching my face a tinge of warmth from an unseen light . . . (25).

Studies of reading disability suggest that the key handicap in learning the skill lies in the inability of the child to enjoy the process. A child who cannot conceptualize time and space dimensions, who is held rigidly by constrictive or diffused ego processes cannot bind or unbind symbols with enjoyment. Reading is an unattractive and often painful task for these children. In addition, a child's lack of enjoyment of reading hinders his development of reading skill which further hampers his functioning. Reading disability, more than any other single handicap, leads on to school failure and frustration.

Competence as a Function of the Ego Processes of Integration

Last and most important, processes of differentiation, fidelity, pacing and expansion need bridges over which each can be harmoniously orchestrated with the others. Integrative processes provide the means by which cognitive-affective transactions can be synthesized into all aspects of the personality structure of the individual. Intellect can, in some instances, be neatly compartmentalized within the personality so that what one knows does not influence what one does. Or what one does is walled off from what one feels.

The basic task of integrative ego processes is to tie symbols into some form of doing. This may appear an easy task since a child is by nature an explorer and examiner. Yet so much of educational processing is passive receiving in the traditional "mug-jug" relationship. The quiet, receptive uneducated mugs (students) receive the juices of knowledge from the large jugs (teachers), who tip over periodically and pour knowledge into all those willing to hold their brains still (pay attention). For effective integration of cognitive-affective transactions to go on there must be a doing by the learning organism.

Integrative ego processes have, in addition to helping the individual cope with the environment, the task of fitting in and organizing its interactions. The ego must make sense out of its transactions by developing a conceptual or metaphorical base from which inputs can be coordinated and related one to another. Each person must find his own style of accomplishing this feat. One needs to keep in mind that variety of integrative styles is normal in a society such as ours and that in this difference lie possibilities and horizons of the future.

Ego Processes and Knowledge

The world of the future will be one in which the ability to manage and be competent in using knowledge will be mandatory. As Machlup (17) and others have pointed out, our society has moved from a society in which the production and distribution of knowledge have supplanted the production and distribution of food as our major activity. In essence our basic human commodity has become knowledge of all kinds. This knowledge industry like a hungry giant is moving so rapidly that in 1963, according to Machlup's estimates, the total outlay for the production and distribution of knowledge came close to 200 billion dollars, up 43 percent in five years.

The American economy and its social system cannot readily be understood unless one is aware of the significance of this change for human competency. Most vulnerable are of course those persons unable to be competent in the use and manipulation of symbols. Automation is not the villain of the future but the large numbers of uneducated persons in our population who can only function in routine, unskilled work. These functions will no longer be available and "good strong hands" will be unable to provide a man a source of competence or wages. As someone said, it takes at least a 12th grade education to supplant a simple machine.

Lastly, the increase of knowledge makes the process of distribution of knowledge a critical one. Such increase makes the processes of digestion and assimilation significant learning skills in light of the huge and growing banquet of data, information, facts, content and concepts which we have available to feed our children. It emphasizes the need for helping children learn processes of healthy data intake, assimilation and use. Without such processes and such learnings, what is taken in can seldom be assimilated; the tendency to fill up on knowledge is a grave danger since our production of knowledge is now endless. The need for balance and growth in learning requires ego differentiation, fidelity, pacing, expansion and integrating processes. Without such processing skills, individual and social competence in a world of knowledge is impossible.

Play

As was indicated at the outset the aim of educational and social competence lies in being able to play, work and love. Although these three competencies will be discussed separately, in reality they are highly interdigitated and interrelated within the person. There seems to be little doubt that, given the freedom to do so, children will play—hard and often. Such play can be considered a rehearsal of competencies needed to survive in the environment and a way of developing the sensory and motor skills which can help the child be competent as a functional biological unit. White (23) proposed the term "effectance" to conceptualize the motivating factors in play which serve to increase individual and social competency. In one of Harlow's experiments (8), young rhesus monkeys caged with their mothers but permitted no play with other monkeys displayed gross abnormalities in adult sexual and social roles. Monkeys permitted daily play with peers but totally isolated from mother showed nearly normal behavior as adults. Although humans and monkeys supposedly came from the same tree, play in human children includes verbalizations and role rehearsal. Children, if left alone, will seek play and playmates as if their life depended on it—and perhaps it does.

The competence to play is the ability to withdraw from one world and social system and enter another. The motivation for such transit is enjoyment and fun. Most delinquents and others with behavior and neurotic disorders are unable to make this shift. I remember attending parties at a residential school for delinquent, emotionally disturbed children and being struck with the inability of the boys and girls to know what to do to have a good time. The alternatives seemed to be fighting or sex "play." As Huizinga (12) points out, no other language has a word which is the exact equivalent of "fun," yet play without "fun" ceases to be play. However, with more time for fun, there seems to be less opportunity or competency for it.

It seems strange that one needs to develop competencies to have fun. If one could remain a child all his life this might not pose much of a problem. But having fun means learning to differentiate between various expressive modes and being able to integrate such behaviors within the personality in a balanced and enhancing manner. For some, all of life is fun and games; for others the stark reality of life is as the Rock of Gibraltar. When the abilities to differentiate, pace and integrate are fully functioning, the individual finds himself able to balance play with work and enjoy both in the process.

Work

While play is a safe and handy way of blowing off steam and gaining temporary victories in the game of life, work is the ability to do something for which one gets paid. This may or may not be all fun but it must be seen as important enough to society to warrant reward and remuneration. About the most important decision made by man is his "choice" of work. Work requires sustained energy and attention; it requires in almost every case managing monotony and repetitious minutia. It requires for human satisfaction some understanding of what one does and its contribution to the scheme of things. Since the major occupation of adult life is work, this should be a kind of activity which enhances self, absorbs psychic and physical energy and offers opportunities for comfortable group feelings even if it requires four coffee breaks a day.

Work as an activity stretches all the way from the teaching of philosophy to plucking dead chickens, from working as President of the United States to being a "roughneck" in the oil fields. All work, however, requires ego processes of differentiation, fidelity, pacing and expansion. To perceive the interests and expanding potentialities in one's work, one must be able to conceptualize its meaning and purpose. Some years ago Goodwin Watson pointed out that the effectiveness of any society is a function of how it gets its floors scrubbed, its windows washed, its hair cut, its clothes laundered, its roads built, its flowers cultivated and its trains run. For persons to gain dignity and development in work, all work must be valued. In societies where all work is valued, all its citizens are valued. Where there is a snobbery about occupations, those persons with low status competencies are often least able to enhance their ego processes in their work. What a person contributes in a job is his way of participating in his society. Without meaningful work this can rarely be accomplished. Money is only one form of payment; the relationship of work to an individual's feelings of self respect and self enhancement is often equally important. To have worked well is to have lived well; to have worked within one's own purposes and competence is a consummation devoutly to be wished for all.

Love

Last, but certainly not least, is the ability to love. To be given the opportunity to define this all conquering passion has boggled the minds of poets, philosophers and scientists. It has been variously characterized as a bowl of cherries, where you find it, just around the corner, and what makes the world go around. As a topic, poets and philosophers have faced up to its existence; only a few behavioral and social scientists have been sufficiently rash to shoot arrows at Cupid.

The essence of love is the ability to encompass within one's ego processes the metaphor of human compassion and oneness of human existence, or as Jessamyn West put it, "love is the struggle to share one's solitude" (22). The way of this sharing is called love. Love is an action, a doing in which four high level abstractions are combined: care, responsibility, respect and knowledge (5). Ego processes which cannot expand beyond a limited self cannot give any of self to others.

In the act of giving, something is born and both persons involved are grateful for the life that is born for both of them. Specifically with regard to love this means: Love is a power which produces love; impotence is the inability to produce love (6).

For educators, one needs to emphasize that love is not a passive acceptance of others but an active helping of others to live. Berlin describes a teacher of a delinquent adolescent who returned day after day to attempt to teach a sullen, hostile, loud-mouthed boy to add and subtract. Despite threats, sullen negativism, malingering, feigned illness and frequent trips by the boy to the toilet, the teacher persisted. Slowly the teacher convinced the boy that he could learn and that he could be helped to do so.

Toughness, not sweet offers of love from the teacher, seemed to do the trick. . . . I am sure you recognize the kind of love that was there—love which has as its focus the well being of someone else. . . (1).*

Love requires knowledge. It is a way of knowing and sensing how one is united with others. Only if one can metaphorically sense this reality can one breach the solitude and separateness of human existence.

Play, work and love then are the goals of effective ego processes. To help children reach these goals is the sum and substance of education.

References

1. Irving Berlin. "Unrealities in Teacher Education." *Saturday Review* 47: 57; December 19, 1964.
2. Robert Blake. *101 Elephant Jokes*. Englewood Cliffs, N. J.: Scholastic Magazines, 1964.
3. Eli M. Bower. "Mental Health in Education." *Review of Educational Research* 32: 441-54; December 1962.
4. J. S. Bruner. "The Cognitive Consequence of Early Sensory Deprivation." *Sensory Deprivation*, A Symposium held at Harvard Medical School. Cambridge: Harvard University Press, 1961. p. 202.
5. Erich Fromm. *The Art of Loving*. New York: Harper & Brothers, 1956. p. 26.

* Printed by permission of the publisher and of the author, Irving N. Berlin, Professor of Psychiatry, Head, Division of Child Psychiatry, University of Washington School of Medicine, Seattle, Washington 98105.

6. *Ibid.*, p. 25.
7. William Fry, Jr. *Sweet Madness, A Study of Humor*. Palo Alto, California: Pacific Books, 1963. p. 220.
8. H. Harlow and M. K. Harlow. "Social Deprivation in Monkeys." *Scientific American* 207: 136-46; 1962.
9. D. O. Hebb. "Drives and Conceptual Nervous System." *Psychological Review* 62: 243; 1955.
10. *Ibid.*, p. 252.
11. Richard Hofstadter. *Anti-intellectualism in American Life*. New York: Alfred A. Knopf, 1963. p. 25.
12. Johan Huizinga. *Homo Ludens*. Boston: Beacon Press, 1950.
13. L. G. Humphreys. "Acquisition and Extinction of Verbal Expectations in a Situation Analogous to Conditioning." *Journal of Experimental Psychology* 25: 294-301; 1939.
14. Marie Jahoda. *Current Concepts of Positive Mental Health*. New York: Basic Books, 1958.
15. Bruno Klopfer. "Personality Diagnosis in Childhood." *Modern Trends in Child Psychiatry*. D. C. Lewis and B. L. Pacella, editors. New York: International Universities Press, 1945.
16. Philip E. Kubzansky and P. Herbert Leiderman. "Sensory Deprivation: An Overview." *Sensory Deprivation*, A Symposium held at Harvard Medical School. Cambridge: Harvard University Press, 1961. p. 221-38.
17. Fritz Machlup. *The Production and Distribution of Knowledge in the United States*. Princeton: Princeton University Press, 1963.
18. Nina Ridenour. *Mental Health in the U.S.* Cambridge: Harvard University Press, 1961.
19. R. Sears, E. Maccoby and H. Levin. *Patterns of Child Rearing*. New York: Harper & Brothers, 1957.
20. Jack Vernon. *Inside the Black Room*. New York: Clarkson N. Polter, Inc., 1963.
21. David Wechsler. "Cognitive, Conative and Nonintellective Intelligence." *American Psychologist* 5: 78-83; March 1950.
22. Jessamyn West. *Love Is Not What You Think*. New York: Harcourt, Brace and World, Inc., 1959.
23. R. W. White. *Ego and Reality in Psychoanalytic Theory*, Monograph II. New York: International Universities Press, 1963.
24. Woodrow Wilson. "The New Freedom." *Essays, Old and New*. Essie Chamberlain, editor. New York: Harper & Brothers, 1943.
25. Richard Wright. *Black Boy*. New York: Harper & Brothers, 1951. p. 283.

New Conceptions of Children's Learning and Development

These are some of the new conceptions which guide our further thought:

From rats to man, we are reexamining our basic concepts of development, learning and motivation.

Children can now be seen as competence-oriented, striving for mastery over their environments.

All aspects of a child's development can be understood as reflecting the nature of his life experiences: (a) Intellectual growth depends upon stimulation, especially in early childhood. Intelligence is not a cause, but a result. (b) Physical, social, emotional development depend upon opportunities to perceive, manipulate, transact with people and objects.

The child is a unified system—what influences one aspect of him has effect upon all of him. He is continually organizing himself and his world. His development proceeds as a "deviation-amplifying mutual causal process."

Instruction is crucial for full development. Intellectual growth cannot be isolated from mental health, a sense of adequacy and self-fulfillment.

3

New Conceptions of Children's Learning and Development

Ira J. Gordon

CHANGES in our view of the world bring with them changes in our view of the child and of man. When concepts and meanings change, data are reorganized and viewed with new insights. In this age of computers and model building, of technology and automation, ideas developed about machine operations often become models for concepts about man. Ideas from the physical and biological sciences are borrowed, sometimes indiscriminately, by the psychological and social sciences and eventually by education.

We can draw an analogy from the changes in thought about the physical world to the thinking now going on, and still to come, about man. The following diagram is merely a model to depict the movement:

Linear Causation Model Man
A mechanistic, fixed, closed system, characterized by
1. development as orderly unfolding
   a. physical-physiological-genetic
   b. socio-emotional: antecedent-consequent
   c. intellectual-fixed

Transactional Model Man
An open-energy, self-organizing system, characterized by
1. development as modifiable in both rate and sequence
   a. genetic-experiential
   b. socio-emotional: field, transactional
   c. intellectual-modifiable

Linear Causation (Cont'd)	Transactional (Cont'd)
2. potential as fixed, although indeterminable	2. potential as creatable through transaction with environment
3. a telephone-switchboard brain	3. a computer brain
4. steam engine driven motor	4. a nuclear power plant energy system
5. inactivity until engine is stoked	5. continuous internal flow of activity
6. additive collection of past	6. organization into a system
7. uniqueness essentially genetic.	7. uniqueness continuously evolving from organism-environment transactions.

The shift in thought is not complete, either in the minds of some behavioral scientists or those whose task it is to educate the young. There is a cultural lag between the ideas developing among some behavioral scientists and their reception and acceptance by teachers and parents.

In order to discuss readily these two models of man, I have labeled the older model, "Linear Causation," and the newer one, "Transactional." Of course, such labels are never completely accurate, but I hope they will be understood as metaphors. One of the main discontinuities is that the home and school still operate to a great extent on an image of the Linear Causation child while the data supporting the changing view accumulate rapidly. This is to be expected; most of us were reared and educated and formed our behavioral concepts in the "Linear Causation" world. These concepts are still useful as explanations of many events, and tend to keep us from becoming aware of the data which are dissonant. Many Americans would accept the following anthropological descriptive statement as representative of their views:

The infant as a potential is thought to be a bundle of largely inherited latent traits of emotional expression and abilities for achieving goals which can only be realized gradually as the child develops and which may be influenced by training and growth. Most of the goals available to children and adults of this community are thought to call for particular skills and a particular personality type, both of which must develop naturally or be influenced to develop out of the latent traits in the infant's potential. Children may have a high or low potential for the development of certain skills or personality traits. The combination of both a high potential and the best environmental influences is thought to be essential to the greatest success in achieving the goals. . . . The belief that the potential is in part concealed leads to a great emphasis on techniques for the discovery and disclosure of the child's potential.

The infant is thought of as possessing innate capacities peculiar to himself which will be revealed in the natural course of his development subject to the influences around him. It is thought that the potential can be developed better if it is known or divined in advance. Divining for the potential is highly developed in the community (14).

This reflects the "Linear Causation" model that you can only "bring out" or fail to use whatever are the latent inherited traits of the child; you cannot really change them. It does contain the recognition of a fundamental concept in the new model, the belief in the uniqueness of the individual.

The source of uniqueness, however, shifts from the genes as sole source in the preceding statement to a recognition that uniqueness is a function of organism-environment transactions in the "Transactional" model. This uniqueness runs through all of the characteristics of the model described in the following section.

From Unfolding Maturation—
Modifiable Development

The first notion is that development itself—in all of its ramifications —is not fixed. That development is modifiable is an extremely important concept. We learned from Gesell, and we thought that we knew, that the child at six would behave in a "six" way and the child at seven in a "seven" way, and the child at eight in an "eight" way. We also knew there were individual differences in rate, so that a particular youngster might reach the six year old "stage" at five or at seven. Nevertheless, this was the scheme; this was the order this child would go through and one simply waited it out.

Research now indicates that this is not necessarily so. It is not so in a variety of ways. It is not so, obviously, in terms of the ages at which things occur because children are now riding two-wheeled bikes at five when we did not think they could ride two-wheelers until they were twelve.

We know that, with better prenatal care, with control over nutrition, with medical developments leading to immunity from childhood diseases, our youngsters are reaching, in motor development, stages much sooner than they did before. Likewise, physiological maturity is being reached much sooner than before.

The evidence from behavioral biology, from anthropology, from animal psychology and child development points to this new concept. From planaria to man, regardless of species, the data lead to the inference of development as modifiable.

The data will be examined in several analytical ways: by viewing the evidence on infrahuman and human subjects separately, and by organizing the data in areas such as biological (including organic, physiologic, motor development), cognitive (emphasizing new concepts of "intelligence") and social-emotional development.

Infrahuman Studies

The lowly rat, long used for learning studies whose findings were therefore often viewed with suspicion by educators, provides us with fascinating information when we either study him in his natural habitat or become more creative in our research approaches. It is clear that the usual laboratory rat, reared in a cage and run through the maze, may be classified in human terms as "culturally deprived."

His cousin, who has roamed free wherever it is that rats roam, can outdistance the laboratory rat in maze learning and complex behavior. The cage is a restrictive environment (2). The series of laboratory researches by Krech and his colleagues has demonstrated that rats reared in environmentally complex environments and subjected to intensive training differ from their littermates in the weight of the cerebral cortex. They differ, also, in the total cholinesterase activity of the brain (cholinesterase being the chemical secretion which seems to facilitate neuron firing in the brain) and in the specific way these secretion levels are distributed in areas of the brain (52).

Further, in investigating whether such differences affected the ability to learn, they found that the timing and extent of experience were important factors. They reported:

> To some degree, the changes induced by an enriched environment can be lost if the animal is placed in an impoverished environment, and to a much greater extent, the originally impoverished animal's brain can be brought to the status of the enriched animal through intensive training on complex problems (30).

Their studies have also shed light on the brain in another way which modifies the older "switchboard" idea in which each part of the brain had a definite, limited function. Experiments with blinded rats, placed in complex environments, showed that these blinded rats could benefit from enriched experience. Even the visual cortex of these rats was modified, "Evidence that the visual cortex participates in non-visual functions" (31). Further, the work of the experimenters led them to test the idea that brain changes were compensatory, that is, the blinded rat overuses other parts of his brain to make up for his deficiency in sight. They conclude, "our present results provide concrete evidence for the often hypothesized possibility of cerebral compensation for blinding" (32).

What does this mean? It suggests that the requirement of usage stimulates structure in the brain, and that all areas of the brain participate, although in differing amounts, in handling the input, coding and response to perceptual-motor stimuli.

When we step up the scale to primates, similar conclusions emerge from the data. Riesen (51) was struck by the fact that visual deficiencies of an organic nature developed in chimpanzees who were reared in darkness. Up to that time, it had been assumed that the optic nerve developed regardless of light stimulation. He concluded that the lack of light affected the normal growth of retina and nerve.

Hunt summarizes some of the other animal studies on deprivation by stating:

> Patterned visual experience appears to be essential for the development of visual perception. . . . Maturation as well as experience plays a role in the acquisition of these visual responses. . . . How permanent and irreversible the effects of visual deprivation are is still unknown as long as no defects within the visual apparatus itself complicates the picture (23).*

As in the rat studies, the nature of the organism-environment transaction governs development. The question of irreversibility is a key one, at the human level, for education. Is it ever "too late to learn"?

The above studies clearly show that environment influences organ function and structural development in infrahuman species. It is a long way from infant rats to humans, but the behavioral biologists tell us the path is continuous and not discontinuous. Although we obviously would not conduct similar experiments on human subjects, field studies of children reared under various conditions, to be reviewed in the next section, show similar results. Before going up the phylogenetic scale again, however, animal studies yield significant data and concepts about the modifiability, through experience, of social and emotional development.

Again we begin with the rat. Studies by Levine (33) indicated that rats who were stimulated in infancy were better able to cope with stressful situations later on. Denenberg and his colleagues found that not only did handling and free environmental experience act to reduce emotionality later in life (9) but also that affecting the emotionality of the mother, "resulted in significant emotionality on the part of the offspring in adulthood" (8).

These studies reveal the modifiability of emotional development in rats; the now classic studies of Harlow's monkeys (18) show even more startling evidence in primates. The research on the effects of wire mothers and cloth mothers led him to conclude that warmth, or tactile communication, was more important than feeding as a factor in "mother love." He reached this idea because when the baby monkey was placed in the situation that he perceived as dangerous, he ran to the cloth mother rather

* J. McV. Hunt. *Intelligence and Experience.* Copyright © 1961 The Ronald Press Company.

than to the wire mother with the bottle on it. Yet Harlow did not stop there. He wrote a followup paper (17), in which he, in effect, said, that when you work with monkeys, you have got to get more monkeys. And, the easiest way to get more monkeys is obviously the way that mankind and the monkey-world have long used. In their attempts to get more monkeys, they found that the monkeys reared on the cloth and the wire monkey mothers did not know how to be monkeys. They did not know what to do except to gaze at each other in amazement. But, Harlow said that they found one male monkey with infinite patience. He finally succeeded with one of the female monkeys, but then they discovered something else. When the new monkey was born, the mother did not know how to be a mother and so she literally beat the baby monkey's head against the floor. The conclusion might be that it takes inter-monkey experience early in life and throughout growing up to learn how not only to produce more monkeys but what to do with them after they are born.

Mason's (34) investigation of the social development of monkeys revealed similar findings: Monkeys reared in semi-isolation with limited opportunity for physical contact with other monkeys did not develop adult social behavior.

Many adult forms of social behavior were absent or appeared in incomplete form.... Aggression and adult forms of grooming and sexual behavior were never observed (35).

The evidence from these animal studies is clear: deprivation of experience modifies social, emotional and organic development; complex environments and training lead to anatomic and physiologic superiority as shown by animals reared in natural habitats and the experimental investigation in rats.

Human Studies of Motor and Behavioral Development

What about humans? Deprivation studies are available from two field settings, each of which demonstrates the modifiability of development by experience. The "Transactional" view of learning and development requires the conceptualization of the importance of perceptual-motor activity. The more traditional view of learning stressed only the motor aspect—the child had to engage in the direct motor behavior in order to master a motor skill such as learning. The earlier tradition also emphasized the role of maturation as a separate dynamic from learning. Walking, for example, in the new view is learned by either watching people walk (perceptual) or engaging in walking (motor). The child has to have experience in either using his legs and/or seeing people use theirs in order to learn to walk.

The best example of evidence is from some orphanages in Lebanon that were studied by Wayne Dennis. He was able to compare children in an infant's orphanage with those who came to a well-baby clinic in the same community. The social class of both the infant institutional children and those who were with their families was similar. For financial reasons, the infants in the orphanage got very little attention during the first year of life. There was one adult staff member for ten children. They lay swaddled in their cribs which had white covering over the sides to protect the child from drafts and which permitted the child to see only the homogeneous white ceiling and those particular adults who came near only for feeding and necessary care. Light, air, food, sanitation were all better than satisfactory; but attention and stimulation were minimal. Feeding consisted, for example, of getting a bottle propped up on a pillow—not very removed from American middle-class infant feeding. The results showed that from the third to the twelfth month the mean score of these institutional children on the Cattell infant scale was 63 and of the comparison children from the same social class, but not institutionalized, 101. No institutional child between three and twelve months of age had a developmental quotient over 95 (11).

In terms of motor development, the classic chart in human development books shows creeping to crawling to walking. These institutionalized children did not go through creeping to crawling to walking. First of all, sitting alone was greatly retarded and in many cases creeping did not occur. Instead they scooted on their bottoms as their way of navigating. They "scooted" on the crib instead of creeping (10).

In the United States, Provence and Lipton (49) conducted a short-term longitudinal study of institutionalized infants. Their results reveal the wide extent of damage to development due to lack of experience. In the case of physical development, first signs of deprivation occurred in the second month when there was a minimal capacity to make postural adjustments to being held or carried.

They reported delays in the control of the head in the pull-to-sit situation, the development of sitting erect, of moving from sitting position, pulling oneself to a standing position, creeping, walking with support, and in walking alone.

However, the infants did not seem behind in lifting the head and chest from the crib mattress in prone, visual following of an object in this position, and rolling from prone to supine.

Since one of the concepts in the "Transactional" model is the selfstimulability, the competence motivation of the child, what happens to this in deprivation circumstances? The researchers report:

> The behavior of institutionalized infants was impressively different from that of children reared by their mothers in respect to autoerotic activity and those other forms of behavior in which an infant acts to stimulate himself in some way....
>
> From four to five months on the changes and deviations were dramatic.
>
> Hand-mouth contacts lessened, thumb sucking disappeared, the mouth took on an appearance of laxity and poor tonus. Toys and other objects were rarely mouthed, sucked, or chewed (50).

Intellectual development as well as physical development is influenced by deprivation. We saw above that exploratory activity is reduced. Even more devastating is what happens to communication, a main source for intellectual development.

> In the last months of the first year the language deficit was even more striking. An occasional mama or dada sound could be evoked after much effort from the adult, but these remained meaningless, nonspecific vocalizations. Altogether there was minimal vocalization of any kind. The repertoire of sounds through which the average baby by this time expresses pleasure, displeasure, anger, eagerness, anticipation, gleefulness, and excitement, or vocalizes something that sounds like a question or interjection was virtually nonexistent. None of the infants had even a single specific word by the end of the first year. Their understanding of the adult's language was also retarded, but less so than was language production (49).

These facts show that experience affects not only the age at which behaviors will occur, but also whether or not they will even occur. And so, experience is a crucial factor for human motor and behavioral development.

Studies of Intellectual Development

Intellectual development even more clearly depends upon experience. Only through active transaction with the world is intellectual structure built.

Intelligence

We are shifting in psychology from a notion that intelligence is fixed and immutable and unchangeable to the notion that we can do something about a youngster's intelligence by the nature of the opportunities for experience that we provide for him. We now believe that intelligence is not a fact, and not a cause of behavior, and not something simply given in the genes. We conceptualize that intelligence is behavior, and behavior comes under environmental control just as much as it comes under biological genetic control. And, therefore, intelligence is changeable.

J. McV. Hunt has forcefully organized and presented data from a variety of sources to demonstrate that "the assumption that intelligence is fixed and that its development is predetermined by the genes is no longer tenable" (24).* His review of evidence "came chiefly from three sources: (a) from the studies of identical twins reared apart, (b) from repeated testing of the same children in longitudinal studies, and (c) from studies of the effects of training" (25).*

In addition to the research work cited by Hunt, A. W. Combs presented similar beliefs from his theoretical position in 1952, when he defined intelligence as the capacity for effective behavior and stated, "the intelligence of an individual will be dependent upon the richness and variety of perceptions possible to him at a given moment" (6). He said, over a decade ago, "If the conception of intelligence we have been discussing . . . should prove accurate, it seems to me to raise serious questions about some of our common assumptions with respect to intelligence and, at the same time, opens exciting new possibilities for the treatment or education of people we have often assumed to be beyond help" (7).

Yet we are only beginning to adopt this concept. In 1964, at the Kennedy Foundation dinner, Kirk talked about the crumbling concept of fixed intelligence. His discussion relates to the changed view of the brain. Recently-devised tests and remedial training techniques which he developed show that mentally retarded children may be close to normal in certain functions and severely retarded in other functions. These tests "assess various 'input' or 'output' deficits of the brain, all or any of which could cause low intelligence scores: They focus on the child's ability to interpret and use different kinds of visual, auditory and tactile experience" (1).

The New York City Board of Education discontinued the use of intelligence tests and has enlisted the assistance of the Educational Testing Service in developing better ways to describe the intellectual capacities of children entering first grade. There are three main lines of attack:

Development of a practical technique with which a teacher can observe and record the ways in which each child displays intelligent behavior, day by day; development of a series of standard performance tasks to elicit intellectual

* J. McV. Hunt. *Intelligence and Experience.* Copyright © 1961 The Ronald Press Company.

behavior from children whose usual behavior in class provides few clues; development of special and differential test materials which will give each child a chance to demonstrate his verbal and quantitative skills in a context that is familiar to him (13).

For the years between the Iowa studies of the 1930's described by Hunt and the search for new ways to measure intellectual behavior by Educational Testing Service in 1964, the California and Fels longitudinal studies have furnished additional data. Bayley's analysis of the California data on the growth of intelligence points up the transactional, "Einsteinian" position. After stating that intellectual growth results from not only inherent capacities but also from the emotional and material environment, from encouragement and opportunity, she concludes: "I suspect each child is a law unto himself" (3).

Sontag and his colleagues explained the individual changes in IQ over the years by attributing such changes to motivation. We can see this position as again illustrative of the emerging view. As I see their main hypothesis, it was of a cyclical, circular-feedback nature. That is, as the child needed to demonstrate mastery of problems (school-type) and to compete intellectually, he would see school as offering this opportunity. Performance in school would be enhanced, and he would learn to do well the type of work we measure on IQ tests. As he learned to do this successfully, he would have less anxiety and approach such tests as challenges. As he approached these tests with this attitude, and with the learned skills, he would perform at a higher level. And so the cycle would begin again.

Let us take just one of the examples given by Sontag and his colleagues:

> Case E. R. shows a child whose score rose from a base of 118 at 3 years to 129 at 4 years. We attributed this to the fact that he was a slow maturer in motor development. Then, after no consistent change for three years, his scores began an ascent which carried them almost to 180. This boy, while not aggressive, is intensely competitive in school, gets great satisfaction from mastery of such subjects as mathematics and chemistry, and spends his free hours absorbed in a book. He depends relatively little on human relationships, either family or peers, for reassurance (56).

These longitudinal studies not only reveal the unique individual patterns of intellectual growth as measured by the standard IQ test, and the role of experience and personal motivation in performance, but also they explode the idea of a fixed adult ceiling on development of intelligence. Bayley and Oden tested adults on the Concept Mastery test, and concluded that their results disagreed with many of the results of earlier studies of adult intelligence. They attributed this to the test, which was designed to differentiate abilities at the upper level, to the fact that their subjects were well-motivated and highly intelligent, and to the longitudinal design used. They state:

The implications to be drawn from our data are that this kind of knowledge and ability improves in superior adults, at least between the ages of 20 and 50. This improvement occurs in all levels of occupation represented, but to a greater extent among the middle occupational classes than in the higher classes. Also, within the professional class, the engineers and chemists, whose training was relatively specific and narrow, evidently broaden their abilities with time, so that on this general type of verbal test their scores attain equality with those of the other professions. This broadening tendency may operate generally among intelligent adults in our culture (4).

These data may all be viewed as emphasizing the role of experience, the transactional "Einsteinian" concept in the development of intellectual behavior.

In summary, the current view might be stated as follows:

First, intelligence is not a single trait carried, like hemophilia, in a single gene. Intelligent behavior has many more aspects than the ability to do academic classroom work. Although our intelligence tests may measure academic ability with a fair degree of accuracy at a given moment, they are not measuring all the dimensions of intelligent behavior.

Second, the behavior of a person is not the result of an additive process, but develops from an organizing, integrating process in which a self-system is produced which represents a new integration of all organism-environment forces.

The evidences concerning the self-system—a person's organized responses—suggest the following conclusions relative to the roles of heredity and environment in intelligence: (a) there is an organic genetic base for intelligent behavior; (b) the actual measured intelligence of a particular person at a particular time, since performance on a test is behavior, is a result of the complex transactions between the organism and its environment up to that point; and (c) performance, therefore, on an intelligence test can be modified by the exigencies of one's life experiences (15).

The last line perhaps should read, in 1966, "on any task requiring intelligent behavior."

Cognitive Development

The studies of Piaget in Switzerland and of Bruner in the United States are widely known. Piagetian theory may be less well known, especially in its developing concepts about the role of experience, because his experiments do not include the manipulation of instructional variables. Vygotsky, in assessing the role of instruction in the development of thought and language, said, "We have given him (the child) a pennyworth of instruction and he has gained a small fortune in development" (60). The problem in cognitive instruction is *when* and *how* to put the penny in.

Piaget's magnificent studies do not address themselves to these questions. He simply gave children particular tasks to do and recorded how they did these. From this, he developed a sequence of stages. One of the studies he did with five-year-olds was to see whether they could make differentiations between what things float and what things sink and whether they could conceptualize about displacement (26). He showed the child a variety of objects and asked, "Does it sink or does it swim?" The child would place the object in the water and make some sort of judgment. Piaget said that five-year-olds could not figure any of this out, and were completely inconsistent. One time they would say the object would float, the next time they said it would sink. They would say it sinks because it is big and the next time they would say it floats because it is big. If they expected it to sink, they would take their hands and shove the object down and make it do what they wanted it to do. This is an accurate description by Piaget of the natural state of affairs. But, does that mean such a state is fixed?

Ralph Ojemann at the State University of Iowa tested this question experimentally. Ojemann's position, which he has taken for 20 years, is that by what we do in the classroom we can modify children's conceptual development. He and his colleague took a group of Iowa five-year-olds to find out whether there was any way to teach these children concepts of specific gravity. The first question they asked the children was, "Do you think it would be worthwhile trying to find out why things float? Why should anybody spend time worrying about why things float?" The children gave three reasons. They said, "We want to know how things work!" (competence motivation at work). They said, ". . . helps us to know what will happen when things are put into water." For example, what happens when you try to place ice cubes in a full glass of water? And then these children, in their apparently inherent wisdom of Bruner's discovery approach, said, "It might help us to find a way to learn about things."

So, they showed the children a plastic ball about 5" in diameter, put it in water where it floated. They asked the children, "Why did it float?" Some of the children said, "Because it's light." Some others said, "Because it's made of plastic," (which is a good Piagetian response). Another said, "Because it's soft"; another said, "Because it's big!" Then the children were shown articles of different weights, made of different things, with different qualities of hardness and softness and bigness and littleness. Two of these items, such as a rectangular piece of iron and a metal jar lid, a plastic lid and a dime, a wooden block and an iron piece, a die and a small glass bottle were put in the water simultaneously and the children watched them. The children very soon discovered from their own observation that you could not simply come to the conclusion on the basis of heaviness or plasticity or softness or size; that their previous explanations produced inconsistent results.

The experimenters went one step further and showed the children that when you put something in water, it pushes the water away. The children watched the water level rise when something went in and then the experimenters asked them, "How much water do you think rises?" The youngsters obviously had no idea of this, so they fixed up a beaker with a spout and filled it up to the spout and put a tube of shampoo in it and caught the overflow in a plastic container. They demonstrated with other objects. The youngsters saw that when you put something in water, it pushes the water away. The youngsters measured and weighed the amount of water and the object. The experimenters then tested the children on the Piaget materials and had the youngsters answer the questions: "Will it sink?" "Will it float?" "Why will it sink?" "Why will it float?"

It was quite clear that these youngsters utilized and understood notions of displacement in the answers they gave to the Piaget material. They behaved at age levels far above the predicted age levels from Piaget's norms. More than that, some of the children had gone through three "stages of concept development" and were behaving at the logical stage of the eleven- and twelve-year-old, although they were only five. Ojemann and Pritchett (42) thus demonstrated that one could influence, by a very careful sequence of experiences, the development of an abstract notion.

The work of Vygotsky (59), and his students in the Soviet Union adds to this picture of the role of experience in concept development. Although written over a generation ago, his book was not translated into English until 1962. Based upon studies of "the level of development requisite for learning the basic school subjects—reading and writing, arithmetic, natural science," he reported, "Our investigation shows that the development of the psychological foundations for instruction in basic subjects does not precede instruction, but unfolds in a continuous interaction with the contributions of instruction" (61). Studies of the temporal relation between instruction and development led him to conclude that "the curve of development does not coincide with the curve of school instruction; by and large, instruction precedes development" (62).

The position taken by Vygotsky was one of intellectual structures built upon deliberate instruction, and then the use of these structures by the developing child to increase his ability to deal with more abstract matters. We note again the cyclical operation. Timing, to Vygotsky, was important. Rather than the concept described in the beginning of this chapter of "divining" for potential, or the traditional idea still held by many teachers of an unfolding concept of maturational readiness, Vygotsky claimed that ". . . The only good kind of instruction is that which marches ahead of development and leads it; it must be aimed not so much at the ripe but the ripening functions . . . instruction must be oriented toward the future, not the past. . . . The school years as a whole are the optimum period for instruction in operations that require awareness and deliberate control; instruction in these operations maximally furthers the development of the higher psychological functions while they are maturing" (63).

These ideas sound familiar to students of both John Dewey and Jean Piaget. They stress that development requires active commerce with the world, and they stress the importance of function. They echo Ojemann's concept of guided experience. The transactional position begins with the child—and builds from there. It stresses openness to experience.

The Higher Horizons project, the Great Cities Program, and the nursery school work of Martin Deutsch (12) all support a view of cognitive development as modifiable.

When the data are reviewed, the transactional nature of development becomes clear.

> This research opens up many possibilities for exploring the role of guided experience in concept development. It offers support for the position that what children are does not necessarily control what children may become. It casts suspicion on procedures which utilize only current knowledge of children as the criterion for curriculum development. It emphasizes the vital influence of the transactional field in effecting future self-development. It removes from us the rigid, ontogenetic barrier to understanding behavior (16).

From Telephone Switchboard to Computer

The studies already referred to, and my interpretation of their meanings, describe what we can see in observable behavior and performance. The question remains: Why does experience play such a crucial role in development? A theoretical position imposes two boundaries upon us. First, it leads us to collect certain kinds of data by studying only certain events in certain ways. Second, it leads us to interpret our findings in keeping with our position. It is only when the data will no longer "fit," or when someone invents a new model or builds a new theory, that we get a reorganization of data and the emergence of new research designs.

In this case, the computer model opened the way. When the brain was conceived of as a telephone switchboard, connections between stimulus and response did not alter the system, the connections were specific, and the line could be disconnected when the call was completed. No call could be made unless the wires were in, and there was no concept that making a call did anything fundamental to any of the wires except those involved in the call. The computer concept, still an analog rather than a "real" representation of the brain, sees the brain as a total active system, with memory drums and feedback mechanism.

The current studies in neurology and physiological psychology by Hebb (20), Miller, Galanter and Pribram (37), Newell, Shaw and Simon (40), all yield data which stress the inherent activity of the brain and its function as an information-processing system. Information received by the brain is stored, not as isolated bits, but as patterns and what Piaget calls "schema," which are analogous to categories, or "concepts." When new sensory inputs reach the brain, they go not only to a particular center, but also the total brain is scanned for similar already-stored data in "memory banks" or memory "tapes." The more information so stored, the more useful the computer becomes. In terms of the living brain, these inputs are organized into patterns or structures.

In an excellent article, written for educators, Pribram challenged the traditional notions of reward and reinforcement and described the brain's operation in terms of the TOTE mechanism:

. . . the fundamental neural organization in control of the association between stimulus and response can no longer be conceived as a reflex arc. On the basis of many new neurological facts, the suggestion has been made that the reflex arc be replaced by a feedback unit which involves (a) Test of readiness with regard to the input, (b) an Operation that seeks to match the test, (c) a re-Test to see whether match has been accomplished, before (d) Exit from control is effected. This TOTE mechanism is ubiquitous—it is essentially a modified homeostat, a mechanism which can control the very input to which it is sensitive. TOTE's are conceived to be arranged hierarchically into Plans, the antecedents of actions. And structually Plans are nothing more than programs, similar to those that guide the operation of computers—well-worked-out outlines such as those used in programmed texts and teaching machines (47).

Piaget's concepts of *accommodation* and *assimilation* also are useful ways to describe how information is utilized. If the data "match" what is already structured, so the child knows how to behave, he merely assimilates the information, and no learning is required. If, however, the information does not match the already developed structure, but is seen by the child as information that requires processing and new responses from him, then he is required to modify his structure to incorporate the new data. He must, in Piaget's terms, accommodate. It is this accommodation which may be seen as taking place at the time which Vygotsky calls the ripening time. The active child utilizes the instruction or information and increases his competence. The child, in effect, uses information to grow on just as his body uses food.

The concepts of accommodation and assimilation are essential, according to Piaget, in order to explain the development of cognitive structure. He states: "Practically, one would have to rely on three principal factors in order to explain the facts of development: maturation, physical experience, and social interaction. But in this particular case none of these three suffice to furnish us with the desired explanations—not even the three together" (43). After discussing why each of these is insufficient, Piaget attributes the explanation to a fourth factor, *equilibration*. In terms used in the beginning of this chapter, this concept is embodied in the model of an open-energy, self-organizing system, always active with the brain functioning in analogous fashion to the computer. Piaget takes the view that development depends on internal factors (maturation) and external factors (physical or social) equilibrating each other:

All exchange (mental as well as biological) between the organisms and the milieu (physical and social) is composed of two poles: (a) of the assimilation of the given external to the previous internal structures, and (b) of the accommodation of these structures to the given ones. . . . The mental equilibrium and even the biological one presumes an activity of the subject, or of the organism. It consists in a sort of matching, orientated towards compensation—with even some overcompensation—resulting from strategies of precaution (44).

He concludes:

Every new problem provokes a disequilibrium (recognizable through types of dominant errors) the solution of which consists in a reequilibration, which brings about a new original synthesis of two systems, up to the point of independence (45).

Motivation is always basic to his concepts of dynamic structure. What is motivating is the push of the child to structure the world. The neurological analog of brain-as-computer and the Piagetian concept of child-as-information-processor can be seen as highly similar. Both models lead away from drive-reduction notions of motivation, and blend with the construct of the child as active and competence-oriented.

The Child as Active and Competent

The Child as Internally Active

The "Einsteinian" model child is conceived as an active, information-seeking and information-processing system. This activity is inherent in his basic biology. His energy is not limited and rationed and the amount of his energy is not a crucial factor as much as the way the energy is directed. The computer analog is most useful here, since the primary purpose of the computer is the handling of information.

The energy is there, it does not have to be stoked from the outside, but its use by the child is the issue. In the current view, the child does not wait to use this energy in order simply to reduce drive. The drive-reduction principle just does not fit this model, because drive is always present, and often children behave to increase the amount of tension and drive they are experiencing. If a drive-reduction view of motivation is inadequate (22),* the current knowledge of the brain as always active (21; 46) leads to a search for the optimum conditions under which this activity is organized for learning and development.

Hebb points out:

> There is no doubt ... that problem-solving situations have some attraction for the rat, more for Harlow's monkeys, and far more for man. When you stop to think of it, it is nothing short of extraordinary what trouble people will go to in order to get into more trouble at the bridge table, or on the golf course; and the fascination of the murder story, or thriller, and the newspaper accounts of real-life adventure or tragedy, is no less extraordinary. This taste for excitement must not be forgotten when we are dealing with human motivation. It appears that, up to a certain point, threat and puzzle have positive motivating value, beyond that point negative value ... risk and puzzle can be attractive in themselves, especially for higher animals such as man. If we can accept this, it will no longer be necessary to work out tortuous and improbable ways to explain why human beings work for money, why school children should learn without pain, why a human being in isolation should dislike doing nothing (19).

* J. McV. Hunt. *Intelligence and Experience.* Copyright © 1961 The Ronald Press Company.

The Child as Competent

The active engagement of the child with his environment, as we have seen, is essential for his maximum development. This active engagement requires perceptual and motor stimulation from the environment, but it also rests on the idea that the child will, when he has not been made apathetic by deprivation, or intensely aroused by threat and frustration, seek out aspects of his environment. It is, in effect, the "full belly and full brain" child (one who has had both biological and intellectual food) who learns the widest range of concepts and develops the more complex cognitive structures.

Two lines of research converge here: one deals with our rediscovery of the competence of the infant, the second is the investigation of competency motivation. The infant as competent should not be read to imply the infant as miniature adult. Nevertheless, some of the earlier notions of neonates as unable to use their senses, as highly unorganized and as inadequate to deal with the world except as a "blob" are under serious attack from a variety of sources. In pediatrics, Smith and his colleagues have shown that "the newborn human, despite significant exceptions, copes with most acquired viral and bacterial infections successfully, associated with the formation of specific antibody. . . . The experimental literature reveals comparable and incontrovertible evidence of neonatal immunological capacity" (55).

Kessen summarized the psychological evidence of the ability of the neonate to make differential responses to a variety of stimuli. He states: *"The young infant is not incompetent,"* or, by Andre Thomas' (58) catching phrase, "The neonate is not a neophyte" (28). He also reinforces the new model of the child by concluding:

> The shift in point-of-view—to set the antitheses sharply—has been from the child who is a passive receptacle, into which learning and maturation pour knowledge and skills and affects until he is full, to the child as a complex, competent organism who, by acting on the environment and being acted on in turn, develops more elaborated and balanced ways of dealing with discrepancy, conflict, and disequilibrium. This shift, I believe, is of incalculable implication and seems to have been accepted to some degree by almost all students of children. Bowlby emphasizes the control by the child in crying and smiling; psychoanalytic theory makes more space for autonomous ego functions; child psychologists dedicated to a learning analysis speak of the child as active; and I suspect Piaget thinks of how he knows it all the time (29).

Competence motivation has been brilliantly summarized by White (64). He coins the word *effectance* to describe the motivation of the child when he is not forced to focus on drive-reduction (hunger, etc.). His view, based upon an intensive review of research, is as follows:

> We are no longer obliged to look for a source of energy external to the nervous system, for a consummatory climax, or for a fixed connection between reinforcement and tension-reduction. Effectance motivation cannot, of course, be conceived as having a source in tissues external to the nervous system. It is in no sense a deficit motive. We must assume it to be neurogenic, its "energies" being simply those of the living cells that make up the nervous system. External stimuli play an important part, but in terms of "energy" this part is secondary, as one can see most clearly when environmental stimulation is actively sought. Putting it picturesquely, we might say that the effectance urge represents what the neuromuscular system wants to do when it is otherwise unoccupied or is gently stimulated by the environment (64).

Why does a child play, for long periods of time, at a single task? We have all seen a youngster so engrossed that the world literally goes on around him. Rather than the old concept of limited attention span for the young child, it is clear that, when the task has meaning to him, he can spend long periods engaged in it. For White, the child does this because he is discovering the nature of the transaction with which he is engaged with the environment. He is finding out what he can do to it, and it to him. White is saying that, given a situation of mild arousal, the child will engage in a wide variety of activities because it is satisfying to him to deal effectively with his environment. He will seek out the more complex tasks over the simpler ones he can already perform.

Simple observation of children on the street or playground shows this: the youngster who has mastered the elements of bike riding tries to do it with "no hands," the prospective little league star chides the novice with the cry that "two hands are for beginners," and the adolescent with the newly acquired driving license is not content merely to drive, but engages in "drag races" and games of "chicken." The adult, in turn, climbs Mount Everest "because it's there."

An experimental investigation by May (36) using nursery school children is but one example of additional evidence. Children given a free choice in the selection of stimuli to play with, overwhelmingly chose the more complex stimuli. Sears and Hilgard, in an excellent review of the role of motivation and learning, conclude:

> Even in the laboratory there is a turn away from deprived states to positive motives, such as activity, curiosity and manipulation, to "hope" rather than "fear" as fundamental (53).

Classroom observations abound in data showing children seeking more complex tasks, inventing work to do, extending themselves beyond the subject matter at hand. Teachers have often seen these activities as "discipline problems." They can now be understood as clues that what is being presented to be learned does not necessarily match either the competence motivation of the child or his present structure. He can, in Piaget's terms, assimilate the material when what he is seeking is opportunity to accommodate to new material.

Man as a Self-Organizing System

In the preceding description of both the theoretical framework and the research evidence, two continuing concepts emerge: (a) Man is an information-processing, organizing open energy system, in constant transaction with his changing environment. (b) Each individual man, because of his own organism and particular environment, creates his own unique contribution to the environment. Although the process of engaging with the environment is common, the stimuli which become information, and the biochemical organization already present at birth to receive and process these stimuli are specific to each person. In this final section of this chapter, these two concepts will be reviewed.

The computer-brain analog and neurological research theory pointed a way to understanding how the brain does this.

We have described the organism as always active, always engaged, always seeking order or meaning. Pribram indicates how neurological structure lends itself to this concept:

The suggestion is that reinforcement is the expression of an organism's tendency toward orderliness; that satisfaction results when a degree of orderliness has been achieved. There is good reason to suspect that the central nervous system is so constructed that order is imposed on its inputs if this is at all possible; if it is not, search continues. . . .

The process of satisfaction is to be conceived as intrinsic to the material ordered and intrinsic to the construction of the nervous system. Education so conceived is truly a process of e-ducere, the art of bringing out this tendency to orderliness (48).

This "push for order" can be seen as serving as a basis for concept-building and categorization. The very nature of the child, neurologically, requires of him that he process information in such a way that categories emerge. What particular concepts, and at what levels of abstraction depend, of course, on input. Schooling which utilizes the child's endeavors to structure his world contributes to competence. Schooling which either tries to impose an order when the child cannot grasp it, or presents masses of data expecting the child to order them as the adult does, may lead to mental indigestion and feelings of incompetence. Concepts such as "inquiry training" and "discovery method" utilize the information processing model, and capitalize on this transactional view. Bruner (5), for example, points out that categorizing reduces the complexity of the environment, allows one to see relationships, and cuts down the necessity for constant learning. He emphasizes, in addition, the concept that categorizing is goal-directed. The latter is particularly crucial for application to schooling.

We have stressed the role of perceptual-motor experience in the development of the child. Simon and Newell make explicit, from a computer model, the interaction of these two processes. They see the organism's survival dependent upon the mutual interaction of perceiving the environment and acting in it. The child not only perceives the environment, he processes the information of what happens as he behaves. He stores, then, both external and internal information. He translates his motor behavior into perceptual symbols—and the development of languages is related to this. Words become symbols which represent perceptions of acts and events. In their words, "Language behavior . . . is highly stylized so that to each distinct language 'act' will correspond an easily perceivable and distinguishable perceptual symbol" (54).

In order to master the environment, to know how to deal with the events which surround and impinge upon him, the child thus engages in behavior that leads to concept attainment. These concepts, or networks of inferences about how to deal with one's self and the world, increase his scope and ability. They give him not only competence, but the feeling of competence.

The longitudinal study conducted by Lois Murphy and her colleagues at the Menninger Foundation led them to conclude:

> In everyday parlance, we say that success breeds success. This is more than a matter of modification of structure by function which constantly contributes to the improvement of skill. What we have seen is a combination of this improvement of skill resulting from the active coping effort; an emergence of belief in or confidence in the worthwhileness of this coping effort which has produced success; the development of a self-image as the child who can master a challenge by his own efforts. That is, triumph or successful results of coping efforts produce motor, affective and cognitive changes which predispose and equip the child for more efforts (38).

Whether or not the child attains both of these is dependent upon the sequences, type and content of experiences provided for him in home, school and community and the unique biochemical organization he brings to these experiences.

The Individual as Unique

To quote from Lois Murphy again, ". . . through his coping experiences the child discovers and measures himself, and develops his own perception of who and what he is and in time may become. We can say that the child creates his identity through his efforts in coming to terms with the environment in his own personal way" (39).

The two key phrases above are *creates his identity* and *personal way*.

As mentioned in the opening section of this chapter, individuality was recognized in the traditional "Newtonian" view of the infant. But, this was a "given." Here, individuality is a creation, an emergent. This individuality permeates every dimension which students of human development and behavior have found measurable. Yet, this uniqueness has not been understood and exploited in the educative process. Traditional learning theory has not only ignored it, but also has assumed that the laws of learning apply to all species. It may be both amazing and amusing to educators to note how naive in this area are these learning "experts."

Any parent or teacher recognizes that children are different. However, as Suppes states, "In spite of the obeisance paid to this tenet (of individual differences in rate of learning) in discussions of curriculum, I consider it the most important principle of learning as yet *unaccepted* in the day-to-day practice of subject-matter teaching in the classroom" (57). Even here, only *rate* is being considered, in spite of the considerable evidence of individuality in cognitive style, personality structure, modes of thinking, self-concept, etc.

These concepts will tend to govern our educational system and impose demands upon us to educate children for such a world. This yearbook, as a whole, addresses itself to the task ahead. I can think of no better chapter ending than this quotation from Earl Kelley:

> Perhaps the most all-inclusive thing we can do for individuality is to learn how to live in a changing universe. The fact of change, unless it is indeed a denial of "fact," seems to be one thing we can be sure of. Those who seek an unchanging base on which to stand will always be disappointed and will always be out of tune with the universe. The immutable, if it could be found, or if one thinks he has found it, calls for rigidity and similarity. To some degree, each individual who stands on the immutable blocks the on-going movement of the creative force which he needs, rather, to facilitate. The person who learns to accept change and looks forward to it has the only security available to humans. He does not know what tomorrow will be like. But he knows it will be different from today. He is glad that this is so, he looks forward to this new tomorrow, and in this, he feels secure. In accepting change, he understands that people are unique and learns to cherish their differences (27).

References

1. *American Psychologist* 19(4): April 1964. p. 293.
2. S. Barnett. *The Rat, A Study in Behavior.* Chicago: Aldine Publishing Co., 1963.
3. N. Bayley. "On the Growth of Intelligence." *American Psychologist* 10: 805-18; 1955. p. 815.
4. N. Bayley and M. Oden. "The Maintenance of Intellectual Ability in Gifted Adults." *Journal of Gerontology* 10: 91-107; 1955. p. 106.
5. J. Bruner, J. Goodnow and G. Austin. *A Study of Thinking.* New York: John Wiley & Sons, 1956.
6. Arthur W. Combs. "Intelligence From a Perceptual Point of View." *Journal of Abnormal and Social Psychology* 47: 662-73; 1952. p. 663.
7. *Ibid.*, p. 671.
8. Victor H. Denenberg et al. "Effects of Maternal Factors Upon Growth and Behavior of the Rat." *Child Development* 33: 65-71; March 1962. p. 71.
9. Victor H. Denenberg, R. Morton et al. "Effects of Duration of Infantile Stimulation upon Emotionality." *Canadian Journal of Psychology* 16: 72-76; 1962.
10. W. Dennis. "Causes of Retardation Among Institutional Children: Iran." *Journal of Genetic Psychology* 96: 47-59; 1960.
11. W. Dennis and P. Najarian. "Infant Development Under Environmental Handicap." *Psychological Monographs* 71: 1-13; 1957.
12. M. Deutsch. "Facilitating Development in the Pre-School Child: Social and Psychological Perspectives." *Merrill-Palmer Quarterly of Behavior and Development* 10: 249-64; 1964.
13. Educational Testing Service *Developments* 12; May 1964. p. 3.
14. John L. Fischer and Ann Fischer. "The New Englanders of Orchard Town, U.S.A." *Six Cultures: Studies of Child Rearing.* B. Whiting, editor. New York: John Wiley & Sons, 1963. p. 922-923.
15. Ira Gordon. *Human Development.* New York: Harper & Row, 1962. p. 29.
16. *Ibid.*, p. 232.
17. H. Harlow. "The Hetero-sexual Affectional System in Monkeys." *American Psychologist* 17: 1-9; January 1962.
18. H. Harlow. "The Nature of Love." *American Psychologist* 13: 676-85; 1958.
19. D. O. Hebb. "Drives and the CNS (Conceptual Nervous System)." *Psychological Review* 62: 243-54; 1955. p. 250-51.
20. D. O. Hebb. "The Motivating Effects of Exteroceptive Stimulation." *American Psychologist* 13: 109-13; 1958.
21. D. O. Hebb, *op. cit.*, 1955.
22. J. McVicker Hunt. *Intelligence and Experience.* New York: The Ronald Press, 1961.
23. *Ibid.*, p. 95-97.
24. *Ibid.*, p. 342.

25. *Ibid.*, p. 19.
26. B. Inhelder and J. Piaget. *The Growth of Logical Thinking.* New York: Basic Books, 1962.
27. Earl Kelley. "The Significance of Being Unique." *ETC* 14: 169-84; 1957. p. 184.
28. W. Kessen. "Research in the Psychological Development of Infants: An Overview." *Merrill-Palmer Quarterly of Behavior and Development* 9: 83-94; 1963. p. 86.
29. *Ibid.*, p. 92.
30. D. Krech, M. Rosenzweig and E. Bennett. "Relations Between Brain Chemistry and Problem Solving Among Rats Raised in Enriched and Impoverished Environments." *Journal of Comparative and Physiological Psychology* 55: 801-807; 1962. p. 806-807.
31. D. Krech, M. Rosenzweig and E. Bennett. "Effects of Complex Environment and Blindness on Rat Brain." *Archives of Neurology* 8: 403-12; 1963. p. 412.
32. *Ibid.*, p. 411.
33. S. Levine. "The Effects of Differential Infantile Stimulation of Emotionality at Weaning." *Canadian Journal of Psychology* 13: 243-47; 1959.
34. W. Mason. "Social Development of Rhesus Monkeys with Restricted Social Experience." *Perceptual and Motor Skills* 16: 263-70; 1963.
35. *Ibid.*, p. 268-69.
36. R. May. "Stimulus Selection in Preschool Children Under Conditions of Free Choice." *Perceptual and Motor Skills* 16: 203-206; 1963.
37. G. A. Miller, K. Pribram and E. Galanter. *Plans and the Structure of Behavior.* New York: Holt, Rinehart & Winston, 1960.
38. L. Murphy et al. *The Widening World of Childhood.* New York: Basic Books, 1962. p. 366. Copyright © 1962 by Basic Books, Inc., Publishers.
39. *Ibid.*, p. 374.
40. A. Newell, J. Shaw and H. Simon. "Elements of a Theory of Human Problem Solving." *Psychological Review* 65: 151-66; 1958.
41. A. Newell and H. Simon. "Computer Simulation of Human Thinking." *Science* 134: 2011-17; 1961.
42. R. Ojemann and K. Pritchett. "Piaget and the Role of Guided Experiences in Human Development." *Perceptual and Motor Skills* 17: 927-40; 1963.
43. J. Piaget. "The Genetic Approach to the Psychology of Thought." *Journal of Educational Psychology* 52: 275-81; 1961. p. 277.
44. *Ibid.*, p. 279.
45. *Ibid.*, p. 281.
46. K. Pribram. "Neurological Notes on the Art of Educating." *Theories of Learning and Instruction,* NSSE 63rd Yearbook, Part I. Ernest Hilgard, editor. Chicago: University of Chicago Press, 1964.
47. *Ibid.*, p. 89-90.
48. *Ibid.*, p. 95.
49. S. Provence and R. Lipton. *Infants in Institutions.* New York: International Universities Press, 1962. p. 118-19.

50. *Ibid.*

51. A. Riesen *et al.* "Chimpanzee Vision After Four Conditions of Light Deprivation." *American Psychologist* 6: 282; 1951.

52. M. Rosenzweig *et al.* "Effects of Environmental Complexity and Training on Brain Chemistry and Anatomy: A Replication and Extension." *Journal of Comparative and Physiological Psychology* 55: 429-37; 1962.

53. P. Sears and E. Hilgard. "The Teacher's Role in the Motivation of the Learner." *Theories of Learning and Instruction,* NSSE 63rd Yearbook, Part I. Ernest Hilgard, editor. Chicago: University of Chicago Press, 1964. p. 207.

54. H. Simon and A. Newell. "Computer Simulation of Human Thinking and Problem Solving." *Monographs of the SRCD* 27: 137-49; 1962. p. 148.

55. R. Smith *et al.* "Development of the Immune Response." *Pediatrics* 33: 163-83; 1964. p. 163-64.

56. L. Sontag, C. Baker and V. Nelson. "Personality as a Determinant of Performance." *American Journal of Orthopsychiatry* 25: 555-62; 1955. p. 561.

57. P. Suppes. "Modern Learning Theory and the Elementary School Curriculum." *American Educational Research Journal* 1: 79-94; 1964. p. 79.

58. Andre Thomas *et al.* "A Longitudinal Study of Primary Reaction Patterns in Children." *Comprehensive Psychiatry I:* 103-12; 1960.

59. L. S. Vygotsky. *Thought and Language.* Cambridge: Massachusetts Institute of Technology Press, 1962. Reprinted from *Thought and Language* by Lev Vygotsky, translated by Eugenia Hanfmann and Gertrude Vakar by permission of The M.I.T. Press, Cambridge, Massachusetts. Copyright © 1962 by The Massachusetts Institute of Technology.

60. *Ibid.*, p. 96.

61. *Ibid.*, p. 98-101.

62. *Ibid.*, p. 102.

63. *Ibid.*, p. 104-105.

64. R. White. "Motivation Reconsidered: The Concept of Competence." *Psychological Review* 66: 297-323; 1959.

A Cognitive Field Theory of Learning

The basis of any profession is a body of theory which enables its practitioners to anticipate the results of acts and events before they occur. The professional worker, by his theories of cause and effect, is equipped to deal with the unique or novel situation and with the individual case which cannot be handled by the routine worker.

The failure of education in the past to develop fully into a profession and to meet the social demands of the time is due to the inadequacy of the folk "commonsense" and reinforcement theories of learning as guides to educational planning. Cognitive field theory, proposed as an alternative, provides a more realistic basis for instructional planning and evaluation and for understanding and dealing with the problems of individual learners.

4

A Cognitive Field Theory of Learning

Donald Snygg

MOST teachers consider psychological theories of learning impractical and use them only when they are needed to justify something the teacher wants to do anyway. This may seem odd to outsiders since teaching is supposedly a profession, that is, an occupation whose members do not conduct themselves by rote and are presumably educated to deal effectively with situations which have never arisen before. Professional work can be done only on the basis of theories of cause and effect which enable the professional worker to predict what will happen in a given case even though the circumstances and situation are completely new.

Knowledge of what has happened in one situation cannot, without a theory of why it happened, enable us to predict what will happen in any other situation if it is different in the slightest degree. If we cannot predict the results of our acts we cannot choose between alternative courses of action or plan new ones. Without a scientific theory of learning, teachers and administrators have to meet new problems with inappropriate routines that were devised long ago to meet other problems or to base their decisions on folk beliefs about learning which, although thoroughly disproved in the laboratories, still pass for common sense.

Teachers are not the only people with professional licenses who tend to drop into the ways of routine workers. As a result of the great surge of scientific discovery, engineers and physicians are having more and more difficulty keeping up with basic theory and are able to remain real professionals only by restricting themselves to narrow fields of specialization. These specialties can be made comprehensible by a narrow band of theory so limited that a busy practitioner can keep in touch with the significant research that bears upon it.

If teachers have not been forced so far on this path of specialization, it may be because the results of teaching are much harder to find and evaluate than the results of engineering or even medicine. Since the primary social purpose of education is a more effective adulthood, the really significant results of teaching do not occur until years afterward. By that time the casual connection between the adult behavior and any classroom events has been covered over by thousands of other experiences and is impossible to trace. As a result, educational innovations tend to be accepted or rejected, not in terms of their results, which are largely unknown, but in terms of the degree to which they fit the beliefs about human nature and human purpose which happen to be in vogue at that time.

Need for Theory

Each of us accepts the validity of methods and devices that fit our view of reality; but methods which do not fit our personal concept of human nature and educational purpose or which we do not feel capable of using are regarded as "impractical theory" and rejected. This makes for a static profession because once an educational practice has come into use it tends to acquire a legitimacy of its own. Teachers who have encountered such a practice from their kindergarten days perceive it as an essential aspect of real teaching. When the practice was new it was accepted because it conformed to the folk belief or the theory of psychology that passed for common sense at the time. Yet once it becomes an accepted part of school practice it no longer needs the sanction of a theory. Instead such a practice comes to serve as a criterion that teachers and parents use for evaluating new educational and psychological theories. Those theories which do not sanction the now hallowed practice are obviously crackbrained, impractical, and for use only in passing examinations and gaining degrees. If this seems exaggerated, consider how the full-arm system of penmanship hangs on in spite of half a century of research on the motor development of children which has negated every assumption on which the full-arm system was based.

If there is now a new interest in theories of learning it is because the tremendous changes in our society have given us the task of preparing children to live in a very different society than we have had in the past. This is a society whose problems we cannot solve and cannot even anticipate. The social and technological changes now sweeping the world are moving so fast that almost any specific fact or procedure taught today will be obsolete before the learner leaves school. As a result, the new subject matter projects take as their objectives the student's discovery of concepts and generalizations and the development of thinking processes, independent learning skills, and creativity. This is not an education solely for an elite class. Within a very few years all routine tasks outside the home will be done by machines, and the adults who have not been helped to attain the conceptual skills and the attitudes of initiative and responsibility required for technical, managerial or professional work will be economically dispossessed, unable to participate in productive work.

We do not know how many people can be brought to the level of intellect, initiative and responsibility that will be required. Nevertheless, the fact that there is already a shortage of professional and technical workers while several million routine workers are unable to find jobs suggests that we must at once begin our search for a solution to this problem.

This new problem requires new methods. The conventional classroom practices were devised at a time when the chief task of the school was the communication of information and the desired outcome was memorization of this information. The fact that the personal qualities required for professional, technical and managerial work are found in many of our graduates does not mean that these qualities are implanted by the schools. The fact that these qualities are seldom found in disadvantaged neighborhoods and are frequently found among children from middle and upper class homes strongly suggests that these qualities are usually learned in the home and not in school. Also, remembering that the general tone and basic methods of instruction were devised long before psychology had become a field of experimental inquiry, when people harbored a great many beliefs about human motivation and learning that have now been disproved or qualified in important ways, it does not seem likely that we can significantly change the product of our schools by just doing more of what we have been doing all along.

It is true that many teachers, unable to see adequate results from their labors, become discouraged time servers, striving only to "make it look good." However, no one who knows teachers can believe that their failure to achieve results which the schools were not designed to achieve is due to any lack in the personal qualities of our teachers. It seems much more likely that we are failing to achieve the new educational objectives of our society because teachers have to base their campaigns, their strategy and their tactics of teaching on inaccurate assumptions about human nature and human learning.

When the free, compulsory public schools first assumed the task of teaching unwilling children what they did not want to know, the first psychology laboratory was still far in the future. On a day to day basis, the classroom teacher in the early public schools, while the mold of tradition was being set, seems to have dealt with the new problems, just as most teachers do now, in terms of one or the other of two prescientific "commonsense" hypotheses about learning, neither of which has stood the test of experimental investigation.

Influence of Frequency Hypothesis

The first of these we shall call the habit or frequency hypothesis. Most people who have attempted to analyze the learning process have begun by noticing that learning, particularly schoolroom learning, often does not occur without a great deal of practice. Logic does not insist that since A commonly occurs before B it must be the cause of B; yet this seems to be an easy conclusion to draw. I once knew a cat which, after cleaning the fish out of the neighborhood pond, succumbed to this logical fallacy and spent most of the next winter sitting on a toilet bowl waiting for fish to appear. In time he gave up his delusion that water causes fish. Nevertheless, many teachers, in spite of their frequent observation of practice that has not resulted in perfection or even progress, persist in the delusion that practice, if continued long enough, will eventually result in learning. "Practice makes perfect" is part of the culture and when all else fails teachers can salve their consciences and satisfy the public by devoting more time to drill, assigning more problems in the workbook, or by lengthening the school day or the school year. The only cost of this type of educational reform is the additional money spent for paper, pencils, electricity and fuel.

Experimental psychologists, like teachers, are children of their culture. As a rule they have started, like the teachers, with the assumption that frequency, repetition, practice or exercise causes learning—that habits are caused by practicing them. Yet few of them have been able to keep that opinion for long. In 1929 Knight Dunlap demonstrated that one way to *break* habits was to practice them (7; 22). He cured typists of their characteristic errors by requiring them to practice the error. He cured children of thumb sucking by requiring them to suck their thumbs. It is reasonable to believe that many children have been cured of piano playing by the same method; and it is quite likely that we have cured quite a few of arithmetic and reading.

Confronted by this situation and by the further observation that much repetition and practice do not result in improvement, a learning theorist must find a "cause" of learning which will either supplement the frequency hypothesis or replace it completely. Looking again into the cultural fund of "commonsense" he finds that learning is also believed to be promoted by rewards and punishments.

The Reinforcement Model of Learning

Teachers have traditionally used praise and blame, prizes, marks, gold stars, certificates of merit, smiles, frowns, detention, and, until recently, the rod, to promote learning. On the commonsense level almost everyone assumes that acts which are punished are less likely to be repeated, that acts which are rewarded are more likely to be repeated. But what is rewarding? Pleasure? And what is punishment? Pain? Perhaps. Yet what is pleasant to one person may be painful to another, a fact well known to most families that have only one TV set. Some pupils work hard for high marks; others try to avoid them. A good conduct award in the fourth grade may cause more misconduct than it prevents. Experiments show that under conditions of high motivation strong rewards and punishments *interfere* with problem solving (1). In some experiments animals given an electric shock every time they made the *correct response* have learned faster than comparable animals who did not suffer shock (21; 13).

The conventional methods of teaching—repetition, reward and punishment—are far from reliable. Practice does not insure perfection. In some cases repetition leads to learning; in others it merely leads to inattention. Rewards and punishments may promote learning or they may interfere with it. The folk theories of learning are very unreliable guides to educational planning.

It is no wonder that many teachers, disappointed in the results of their attempts at professional planning, lose faith in themselves and fall back on a ritual of routine practices copied from the teachers they respect.

In an effort to build a more reliable model of the learning process, present-day S-R psychologists have dropped the terms "reward" and "punishment" in favor of positive and negative "reinforcement." Although many people assume that "reinforcement" is merely a technical name for "reward" and think of the two as synonymous, the shift from reward to reinforcement is a very significant one. Reward theory assumed that "rewards," acting independently, will strengthen the pupil's tendency to perform the act which has been rewarded. "Reinforcement" implies a vaguer theory of causation. Reinforcement is merely defined as whatever strengthens the tendency for a particular response to follow a particular stimulus. That is, a "reinforcement" is identified only by its consequences. In effect, the S-R psychologists, having decided that at this time no one has enough information to tell why reinforcement takes place, have decided to quit worrying about it and to go to other problems. "Reinforcement" is not reward. It is simply the name for a hypothetical process and offers no explanation of the process.[1]

This leaves the teacher who wishes to use reinforcement theory in a bad situation. Without a theory of what causes reinforcement he is unable to make any plans for achieving it. The most anyone can do is to give the practice lip service and go on using the old folk theories of repetition, reward and punishment as teachers have always done. As a matter of fact a good many psychologists do this, too, but they have one advantage in the laboratory that the teacher does not have in the classroom. The psychologist knows by experience that starving a rat or pigeon down to 75 percent of normal body weight provides a situation in which the presentation of food very frequently results in reinforcement. So, if he wants to, he can forget that problem and go on to study other aspects of learning. Public sentiment fortunately prevents the application of this empirical discovery to schoolchildren.

Unquestionably the stimulus-response model of learning is by far the easiest model on which to base research. In the past fifty years an overwhelming majority of learning experiments have used the S-R pattern. Indeed this pattern has had such a monopoly on the field that some psychologists call it "learning theory" implying that no other conceptual model is possible. Others concede that other conceptual models for learning are possible and may even be useful but believe that only the S-R can be scientifically legitimate. This, of course, is nonsense.

The only scientific criterion for judging any theory is its usefulness in predicting previously unknown facts and thus making possible new and better practices. By this criterion the S-R model of learning has failed to justify itself. For fifty years it has almost monopolized the facilities of the experimental laboratories and during that time this theory has not led to the invention of a single educational technique which was not already in use and originally derived from the prescientific folk theories of exercise, reward and punishment. When it has been pos-

[1] To be accurate, not all S-R psychologists accept the concept of reinforcement. Guthrie was able to construct an S-R theory which did not use this concept.

sible to apply S-R theory to educational practice the results have not validated the model. The early teaching machines were expected to open a new era in education by making possible the immediate reinforcement (by showing when the answer was correct) to the student's response (writing an answer to the stimulus question). A number of research studies have found that their subjects learned just as well when they did not write an answer (make a response) to be reinforced at all but simply read the machine tape, as when they read a book (12; 19). Generally these students learned more in a given length of time than the students who followed the standard procedure because they did not have to spend time writing. Other experimenters found that some of the best learners in their experiments were the subjects who made the most mistakes and consequently had had the fewest correct responses reinforced.

The reinforcement S-R model of learning cannot serve the needs of education in this century because it is a model for teaching that which is already known. The task of the teacher using reinforcement theory looks, on the face of it, very simple. His task is to set up a situation in which the student will make the desired response and then, without delay, the teacher must see that something happens which will result in that response being reinforced. This does not look hard to an experimental psychologist who has a supply of feed and a hungry pigeon or rat in a box where it has only two possible choices. This task, however, is probably impossible for a teacher who is in a room with thirty children with widely differing interests, abilities and personal problems. The essential limitation of the model is that the teacher has to decide what words or actions should be reinforced. An act which does not conform to the teacher's idea of what is good, proper and effective, a problem solution which differs from the solution he would make, cannot be reinforced. In such a situation, conventional, routine behavior is going to be reinforced; creative and inventive behavior is not.

If reinforcement theory could be put into educational practice, it would only serve to teach what is already known, to promote conventional, conforming behavior, to prepare pupils to live in a world exactly like the one in which they are educated. In a world changing as rapidly as the world is changing now, in which we cannot teach our children the answers to their future problems because we cannot even anticipate the problems, an education based on reinforcement theory would be an education for obsolescence. If what is desired is a creative, adaptable citizen, able to deal with problems his teachers could not have envisaged and with problems they were unable to solve, another model for learning must be used.

One of the strong reactions against the reinforcement model for learning has come from the people who have been developing the National Science Foundation projects. They have been confronted with the problem of teaching what Bruner (2) has called the structure or logic of a subject matter area. Although the concept of subject matter structure is not new, most teaching in American schools has conformed to the stimulus-response model of Thorndike's early "pre-belonging" theories. Items of information are taught separately and rewarded or, as in Skinner's learning machine, "reinforced" separately. The scientists given responsibility for the NSF projects have insisted that teaching items of information is not the way to teach science. Each area of science, they insist, is made up of a structure of interrelated concepts and conceptual models which gives meaning to the separate facts and thus makes possible the deduction of new ones. Isolated facts, without a theory to unify them, do not tell us what to expect in new situations and consequently do not equip the student for success in any but routine situations where other people have already worked out the answers. If this is true, the first qualification of a teacher should be the ability to practice the science he is teaching. Yet he must also understand a great many things about teaching, including the answers to some questions about how concepts are taught, that people are just beginning to think about.

Cognitive Field Theories of Learning

Psychologically, the concept of subject matter organization fits into a general concept of cognitive organization and motivation which is being developed by a number of psychologists. Ausubel, Combs, Festinger, Heider, Rogers, Snygg, and Taba and many others have contributed to the general theory. At the present time the work of Piaget (15) is most influential in providing a common ground for definition of problems. While the proponents of the cognitive approach differ from one another in minor ways they have, under the influence of Gestalt psychology, Tolman's cognitive behaviorism, Lewin's field theory, and a number of other sources, come to fairly close agreement on their model of learning. However the particular version which follows is that of the author.

It is assumed that an individual's behavior is always appropriate to his phenomenal field, perceptual field, cognitive field, conceptual field or cognitive structure. Snygg and Combs (17) define the phenomenal field as the universe, including himself, as perceived by the individual at the instant of action and postulate that all his behavior is determined by and appropriate to the field at that instant. If his field changed, he would change his behavior to conform to it. The purpose of education is to promote more effective and realistic behavior. This is done by helping the individual to achieve a more fruitful and realistic concept of himself and of the universe.

The term "field," as used by various writers, implies an organized whole which behaves in such a way as to maintain its organization. Piaget, as interpreted by Taba (20), believes that "the individual in 'any cognitive encounter with the environment' of necessity organizes the objects and events into his existing cognitive structure, and invests them with the meaning dictated by that system." He perceives each new phenomenon in terms of an already existing conceptual framework, and new phenomena have meaning only to the extent that they can be fitted into the patterns of concepts and relationship that already exist in his mind. Festinger (9) postulates that individuals will always perceive in such a way as to reduce the dissonance in the cognitive field; Snygg (16) that the immediate purpose of all an individual's behavior, including his behavior as a perceiver, is the maintenance or organization of his individual field.

Generally speaking, a learner will accept into his field anything which fits what he already believes but there are two qualifications: (a) in order to be perceived or assimilated an object or event must be necessary to the field organization; (b) assimilation of an event involves what another person, looking at the event from the point of view of his own perceptual field, would call distortion. Any item's value and meaning are aspects of its function in the perceiver's particular field at that particular time.

If these conclusions are correct, any attempt to make a really significant change in a student's field by verbal means seems foredoomed to failure. Lectures, reading assignments, and class discussions may give students the raw material for filling in gaps in their perceptual worlds and for rationalizing the preconceptions and prejudices they already have. Such methods by themselves, however, are not at all likely to cause a radical change in any student's concept of reality. We can assume that each external event is perceived, if at all, in such a way as to cause the least possible change in the student's field. The words of a lecturer will only rarely be relevant to the private reality and personal problems of the students he addresses and are very easy to ignore.

The usual plan for overriding this implacable mechanism for protecting the student against the intrusion of dissonant perceptions is to disorganize his field by threats of failure and humiliation in the hope that he will try to remove the threat by learning the required material.

The results are frequently far from what teachers and parents intend. All teachers are by now aware of the cheating and the defensive changes in self-concept and personal values that may result among "poor" students. More attention should be given to the problem of the "good" student who learns the required material for examination purposes but keeps it from entering and changing his view of reality by dividing his field into two parts, "reality" and "school," the latter having nothing to do with real life. This is the game that has given the word "academic" its connotation of impractical futility. The bright people who have used this defense and made a success of school without changing their concepts of reality feel more competent in "school" than in "real life." Apparently many such persons become teachers. We often see teachers and children playing the school game together, equally unaware that the concepts they discuss have anything to do with life or action.

Unfortunately for our efforts to write examinations that are easy to mark, the ability of a student to write the verbal definition of a concept does not prove that the student has the concept. A few years ago I had in one of my classes a student from India who was eager to see snow. She had read about snow, she had seen pictures of snow crystals, she had seen snow on the tops of distant peaks in northern India, and she had taught Indian children all about snow. Then one morning in early December she walked out of her dormitory to find the air full of fluttering white objects. "Oh!" she exclaimed, "What kind of insects are these?" The verbal definition is the last stage of development of a concept and the concept will be perceived as part of reality only when it has been discovered by the student as part of the reality of his own experience, in his own perceptual field.

Any concept, no matter how well expressed, can only be accepted if it fits the student's own cognitive field. In conventional terminology he is "ready" for such learning but the trouble is that if he is that ready there is not much change in his field. On the other hand, if the fit is imperfect the law of least change operates with distressing results. If the dissonant statement is heard at all, the most economical way to deal with it, that is to keep the change in the student's field at a minimum, is to accept it as a statement of fact which has no relevance to the real life of the listener. Probably most lecture and reading material is disposed of in this way. Unfortunately for the student, this denial of personal meaning insures that the material will not be available when he needs it later. He may, of course, perceive the statement as pertinent to the school sector of his life, particularly the next class meeting. But since the material is perceived as mainly pertinent to the next recitation, it is not available after that date and has to be reinstated for the examination by cramming. After the examination, as we all know, it is lost forever.

In the sense in which I have been using the term, a concept is defined as "a general meaning, an idea, or a property that can be predicated out of two or more individual terms" (8). Whether he can express it verbally or not, an individual cannot be presumed to have a concept unless he is able to discover and identify new items which fit the concept. Tests for concepts, to be valid, must be performance tests which require applications of the concepts in new situations. Since concepts are cognitive, and since "cognitive" is often mistakenly equated with "verbal," it should be pointed out that when people develop concepts the formulation of a verbal definition has to be the last step in the process, and that it is probably not an essential one. A great many people who have developed their own concepts and who use them with precision have never had the need to put them into words and may not even have the ability to do so.

Can anything be taught by verbal means? Yes, if the words can be used to upset the student's perceptual field or if the student can use them to organize it. Learning takes place when the field is so disorganized that a new perception, which would ordinarily be ignored, is sought out as a means of restoring or enhancing the organization. New ideas are accepted only in situations where their rejection would cause even more change than their acceptance. We postpone the perception of discrepancies as long as possible but once their perception is forced upon us we must go on to a new organization and actively seek a means of achieving it. Piaget calls this extension of the field to fit new demands "accommodation." Taba (20) illustrates it by the example of a child who, having thought of measurement as an operation done with a yardstick, is confronted with the problem of measuring a volume of water and has to enlarge his concept of measurement.

A Cognitive Field Model of Learning

As a pattern for promoting learning from this point of view we can use the following model. It is applicable to both learning and problem solving and is a modification in cognitive field terms of one proposed by Cronbach (6).

Step 1. Awareness of a need for greater organization (e.g., hunger, anxiety).

Step 2. Search of the phenomenal field for some means of achieving organization (e.g., food, self-assurance). This or some means of approaching it is differentiated in some degree as $Goal_1$.

Step 3. Simultaneous search of field for means of reaching or achieving the goal. The tentative path is differentiated into sub-paths. *Perception of Problem$_1$*.

Step 4. Act$_1$ begins, appropriate to this perception$_1$.

Step 5. Perception of Results$_1$. If the act or series of acts achieves the goal, no significant reorganization or change of the field is necessary and, as a consequence, nothing is learned.

Step 6. If, however, the results are not as expected or hoped, the situation is reexamined. This results in *Perception of Problem$_2$*.

Step 7. This new and more highly differentiated perception of the situation results in new *Act$_2$*.

Step 8. Perception of Results$_2$. If the new results are those sought, the search-act-evaluation process in the problem area is terminated and the individual shifts his attention to problems elsewhere.

Step 9. If the desired result has not been attained, the search-act-evaluation process goes on until a new perception of the problem makes possible the attainment of the goal or until the learner differentiates another goal as a more practical way of satisfying his need. The new perception of the problem is what has been learned.

It will be noticed that this concept deposes both practice and reinforcement as "causes" of learning. Each repetition of the problem gives the pupil an opportunity to gain a clearer and more accurate perception of the situation but it does not guarantee that he will either wish or be able to take advantage of the opportunity. Practice, in other words, gives an opportunity for learning but does not cause it. "Reinforcement" is not needed to stabilize the successful response. The learner merely stops reinterpreting the situation because further change in that aspect of the field is unnecessary.

The model is as applicable to skill and nonverbal learning as to concept discovery and problem solving. The object of search in motor learning is the differentiation of more effective muscle feelings, visual and motor cues, and rhythm and breathing patterns. As in cognitive learning, the process is one of increasing differentiation of the total situation during which the perceived task is differentiated into more and more subtasks until the cues essential to solution are discovered.

Transfer of learning from one situation to another occurs when

1. The learner perceives the two situations as similar.

2. When he perceives a solution to one problem as applicable to part of another problem.

3. When he acquires new perceptions of himself or of the world at large which are applicable to both or all situations.

Education for the unforeseeable (an awkward problem for association systems) is thus seen as possible. Personality and character training, which by connectionist theories would have to be achieved by a large number of separate learnings, are achieved by helping the individual to perceive himself as an accepted, responsible, valuable member of society and by helping him learn the knowledge and skill adequate for the role.

Implications of the Cognitive Field Theory

Assuming the validity of the steps in cognitive field theory listed, teachers and curriculum planners can draw the following implications:

1. (*Goals*) The primary function of the teacher is to help the students to discover problems that demand their personal attention. Giving students answers to problems they do not have short-circuits the whole process of learning by making exploration and reality testing by the students unnecessary and the problem (whose solution they are taught) unimportant. Fundamentally, the curriculum aids the student, not by giving him the answers to problems that he does not have, but by helping him to discover new and more fruitful objectives in his personal campaign for feelings of greater worth and value. Students must be protected from ready-made answers which make their own consideration of the problem unnecessary.

This requires a flexible curriculum, in the sense that the goals it presents must be appropriate to the personal value system, the self-concept, and the present understanding and skill of the student if he is to accept them as personal goals, to be pursued seriously and with persistence.

This requires the teacher to think of himself as a learner who needs to explore his students' perceptions of the subject and of themselves so that he can give special treatment to the individual. This requires a classroom setting in which the student is free to explore and express his own perception of the situation without fear of humiliation or reprisal so that the instructor can see the consequences of his own acts (18). Since each individual selects his goals from among those that seem valuable and feasible to him, different students will have very different goals. And in exploring the situations for the means of reaching their different goals they will make very different discoveries.

2. (*Interpretation*) The teacher uses this knowledge to arrange a situation in which the student will have a better opportunity to solve his problem without direct instruction. This may be done by providing the required tools, by providing the necessary experiences and conceptual models, and sometimes by removing extraneous factors from the situation so that the essential aspects can be more easily differentiated.

A curriculum based upon perceptual field principles will have to assume that the teacher is a professional worker in the true sense and is equipped, as routine workers are not, with a background of professional theory which enables him to deal with unique cases and with situations that have never before arisen.

Different students with the same goal will still interpret any situation differently since they approach it with different field organizations. As a result, group discussions are valuable if the members of the group are willing to learn from one another. This applies to the teacher as well as to the students. He must not assume that his interpretation is the only one that is possible or useful. If one of our purposes is to help people become creative and capable, the validity of other ways of solving a problem and, in some cases, of other solutions must be accepted by the teachers.

3. (*Act*) The validity of our concepts and our perceptions can only be tested by acting on them. In experiments on the effect of minimal stimulation, when people were kept lying in the dark, in soundproof rooms, unable to touch or hear anything, they soon began to have hallucinations, to see and hear objects that were not present. The only way to find the extent to which a perception represents reality is to act upon it. It is in this area of reality testing that our schools are most inadequate.

It is essential that the curriculum and the school situation give the student the opportunity to test his perceptions of reality by acting on them. Ideas not put to the test of action are, quite properly, perceived as doubtful, as play money for tender in examinations but not to be trusted in real life where we are playing for keeps. The failure of students to apply their verbal learnings from the classroom to their behavior outside the classroom is due, from the perceptual field point of view, to the fact that these "learnings" have never been successfully validated by use and thus remain merely something to talk about.

A curriculum based on perceptual field principles will provide many opportunities for the student to put his ideas to the test of action so that he will discover and correct his misconceptions as soon as possible and so that he will gain the confidence required to act on his perceptions and concepts and to make them the basis for his further thinking. In a modern physics curriculum the students do not just talk about gravity, they measure it by methods they understand (because they have helped develop them) (18).

4. (*Perception of Results*) A man spearing fish for the first time sees his spear dart harmlessly by the fish and immediately changes his perception of the situation. An act which does not achieve its expected

result automatically causes a change in the behaver's perceptions of the situation *provided* he is able to see the result. If he cannot discover the results of his act he cannot tell whether his interpretation of the situation needs modification or not. An act, without knowledge of its results, cannot benefit learning.

Papers unread, questions not answered, suggestions not made leave the student in the role of a man trying to spear fish in the dark, not knowing where his spear is going nor where the target is. Better provision for the immediate marking of papers, emphasizing what is successful and what is ingenious and promising at least as much as what is poor, and better facilities for self evaluation by students are greatly needed in most schools. Most important is the invention of new opportunities for students to see the results of their work. Teacher evaluations are obscure, based upon other standards and values, and often threatening because their basis is not understood. Poor students easily rationalize them away by telling themselves that the evaluations are by people with peculiar values. This does not hurt the teachers but it does hurt the pupils by removing them from the teacher's sphere of personal influence.

In learning, the important evaluation is the one made by the learner. To make this evaluation as realistic as possible, he should see the results in as realistic a situation as possible and in a social situation where he feels respected and valued so that he will feel less need to protect himself with rationalizations and excuses.

If this view of learning is valid, learning is a process of exploration and experimentation. Making the class period a testing period and the marking of daily recitations inhibit exploration and learning because the student can take no chances by exploring and trying to learn in a marking situation in which the obvious need is the need to please the teacher.

In the teaching of science, laboratory exercises should be genuine experiments with explicit significance for the student. They should be true explorations of unknown territory and at least part of the procedure should be devised by the student. Ingenious writers might be able to apply the general idea to the social sciences. In mathematics the invention of alternative methods should be encouraged and even required. Following in someone else's footsteps does not help us to solve problems. It merely teaches us to follow footsteps.

Both perceptual field and reinforcement theories suggest that immediate knowledge of the results of an act is essential to learning. Field theory suggests that the essential factor is the learner's discovery of the relation between the cause and the result. For this purpose a teacher's evaluation of the results cannot be an adequate substitute for the student's own perception of the consequences. Strictly speaking, the teacher can tell the student only about the teacher's perception of the results and this may not be pertinent to the student's evaluation of the results when the teacher is not present. This brings back, in a new form, the distinction between intrinsic and extrinsic rewards and suggests that the distinction may be more important than we have thought (18).

The objections to the traditional emphasis on evaluation by the teacher may be summarized as follows:

a. Emphasis on the teacher's evaluation leads the student to concentrate more on making a good impression than on finding an effective solution.

b. Since the instructor's criterion for the evaluation of student papers and recitations must be his own perception of the situation, independent, creative and unorthodox thinking is unintentionally discouraged.

c. Since the teacher's cognitive field necessarily differs from that of the student, his suggestions for revision are often unconvincing to the student.

d. Limitations of language and experience make the transmission of individual perceptions and meanings very risky and inadequate.

e. The tradition of verbal examinations, by focusing attention on the verbal interpretation of problems instead of on appropriate action tends to make education a verbal game and to make teachers and students men of words, incapable of action.

All of these considerations point toward a need for greater cooperation between students and teachers in selecting and defining problems, for more situations where individual interpretations can be put to the test of action, and for the provision of facilities, materials and resources to make this possible.

5. (*Reinterpretation*) Generally the change in the learner's perception of a situation is in the direction of increased awareness of details and in breaking the total problem into a number of sub-problems and related steps until he can relate this situation to a model or concept he has already developed. As long as the teacher does not take over and impose his own solution, based on his own perceptions, he may safely call the student's attention to some details in the situation as factors the student might want to consider.

It is essential, however, that the student not be led to feel that the teacher has taken over the problem or that his own work is unnecessary and valueless. Above all, the student should not be led to become dependent on the teacher. The teacher should not interfere to prevent the student from making mistakes.

One of the most striking implications of perceptual field theory is the function this theory assigns to error. From this point of view learning does not take place unless the learner finds that he has made a mistake or would have made a mistake, that is, unless an act enlarges his perception of the situation by giving rise to results he did not anticipate. The optimum situation for learning is not one in which the learner will make no mistakes, as in current reinforcement theory. Rather, optimum learning takes place in a situation which allows the learner to test his ideas under conditions in which the results are immediately apparent.

Level of Difficulty

One of the most unconventional implications of the perceptual field theory is the push it gives toward more difficult curricula. Contrary to the general opinion among teachers, which postulates that all failure is detrimental because it causes frustration and thus either aggression or withdrawal, and contrary to the opinion of reinforcement theorists, which tends to assume that material should be so easy that all responses to it will be "correct" (so that they can be reinforced), perceptual field theory suggests that *the optimum level of difficulty is one which allows the student to win success after difficulty.*

If our basic goal is indeed a greater feeling of personal worth and value, tasks which require little talent or effort are bound to be unrewarding and boring and to be as unproductive and harmful from an educational point of view as are problems that are completely beyond the current capacity of the student. Most teachers and educators are well aware of the latter danger; fewer seem to have considered the first.

The success or failure of the implementation of current curricular developments into effective practice may well depend upon the degree to which both curriculum planners and learning theorists will translate the implications of the perceptual field theory into a rigorous upgrading and strengthening of the quality of the educational program throughout the entire school span (18).

Although the field approach is just beginning to come into use as a conceptual model for education, it has already exerted a strong influence on our ideas about pupil readiness and the nature of the IQ. Readiness for a particular experience, from this point of view, depends not only on the student's physical maturity but, even more, on the character of his perceptual field which determines his ability to assimilate new stimuli and the meaning he will ascribe to them. "Readiness" is something which can be achieved through educational experiences. Unless physical inadequacies make experiences impossible or meaningless, readiness for intellectual achievements can be promoted by appropriate experiences. And in the case of children living in environments where the appropriate experiences are not available, waiting for readiness is waiting for accidents that are not likely to happen.

It is now clear that a low IQ may be due, among other things, to the failure of the home and neighborhood to provide the preschool child with the incentives and experiences that prepare most middle-class children for involvement in some degree of abstract thinking and intellectual interests (3; 11). During the great IQ controversy of the 1930's the professors' children in the University of Minnesota and the University of California nursery schools showed no significant change in IQ; but in Iowa City, where the nursery school children came from all sections of the community, there was a significant rise.

A home in which children are taught to approach the world as something to be mastered, where they learn to perceive the world as extended in space and time and to govern their actions by what is beyond the horizon and in the remote future is probably doing all that the very best school can do for young children now. The child whose home and neighborhood do not provide the kinds of opportunities for experience that lead him to see himself as an active participant in shaping the future has to get these experiences elsewhere; and unless he gets them before he enters the regular school program the experiences he gets there will be perceived as having no meaning for his own life.

The danger is that the country is embarking on a great program of preschool education for disadvantaged children before we know what opportunities for experience to give or how to give them. The purpose of teaching three-year-olds to read, if this is tried, should not be to hasten their graduation from school. The purpose is to help them to perceive themselves as individuals who can learn and to discover that their thoughts have significance before their homes and their community have taught them otherwise. It is obvious that applying present day first grade methods to three-year-olds will not automatically achieve these ends. In fact such methods may make matters worse by teaching the children at the age of three instead of at the age of six that they are incompetent and that school activities are meaningless.

References

1. H. G. Birch. "The Role of Motivational Factors in Insightful Problem Solving." *Journal of Comparative Psychology* 38: 295-317; 1945.

2. J. S. Bruner. *The Process of Education.* Cambridge: Harvard University Press, 1961.

3. A. W. Combs. "Intelligence from a Perceptual Point of View." *Journal of Abnormal and Social Psychology* 47: 662-73; 1952.

4. A. W. Combs, editor. *Perceiving, Behaving, Becoming.* Washington, D.C.: Association for Supervision and Curriculum Development, 1962.

5. A. W. Combs and D. Snygg. *Individual Behavior.* New York: Harper & Brothers, 1959.

6. L. J. Cronbach. *Educational Psychology.* New York: Harcourt, Brace and World, Inc., 1954.

7. K. Dunlap. *Habits: Their Making and Unmaking.* New York: Liveright Publishing Corp., 1932.

8. Horace B. English and Ava C. English. *A Comprehensive Dictionary of Psychological and Psychoanalytical Terms.* New York: Longmans, Green & Company, 1958. Used by permission of the publishers, David McKay Company, Inc.

9. L. Festinger. *A Theory of Cognitive Dissonance.* Stanford, California: Stanford University Press, 1957.

10. H. F. Harlow. "Mice, Monkeys, Man and Motives." *Psychological Review* 60: 23-32; 1953.

11. J. McVicker Hunt. *Intelligence and Experience.* New York: Ronald Press Co., 1961.

12. P. M. Lambert, D. M. Miller and D. E. Wiley. "Experimental Folklore and Experimentation: The Study of Programmed Learning in the Wauwatosa Public Schools." *Journal of Educational Research* 55 (9): 485-91; 1962.

13. K. F. Muenzinger. "Motivation in Learning I. Electric Shock for Correct Response in the Visual Discrimination Habit." *Journal of Comparative Psychology* 17: 267-77; 1934.

14. R. E. Ripple and F. P. Hodge. "A Comparison of the Effectiveness of a Programmed Text with Three Other Methods of Presentation." *New Directions in Educational Research.* Albany, N. Y.: Educational Research Association of New York and State (N. Y.) Department of Education, 1963. p. 61-63.

15. R. E. Ripple and V. N. Rockcastle, editors. *Piaget Rediscovered.* Ithaca, N. Y.: School of Education, Cornell University, 1964.

16. D. Snygg. "The Need for a Phenomenological System of Psychology." *Psychological Review* 48: 404-24; 1941.

17. D. Snygg and A. W. Combs. *Individual Behavior.* New York: Harper & Brothers, 1949.

18. D. Snygg. "A Learning Theory for Curricular Change." *Using Current Curriculum Developments.* Washington, D. C.: Association for Supervision and Curriculum Development, 1963. p. 109-15.

19. L. M. Stolurow and C. C. Walker. "A Comparison of Overt and Covert Response in Programmed Learning." *Journal of Educational Research* 55: 421-29; 1962.

20. H. Taba, S. Levine and F. E. Freeman. *Thinking in Elementary School*

Children. Cooperative Research Project No. 1574, U.S. Office of Education. San Francisco, California: San Francisco State College, 1963.

21. E. C. Tolman, C. S. Hall and E. P. Bretnall. "A Disproof of the Law of Effect." *Journal of Experimental Psychology* 15: 601-14; 1932.

22. G. Wakeham. "A Quantitative Experiment on Dr. K. Dunlap's 'Revision of the Fundamental Law of Habit Formation.'" *Journal of Comparative Psychology* 10: 235-36; 1930.

23. R. W. White. "Motivation Reconsidered: The Concept of Competence." *Psychological Review* 66: 297-333; 1959.

Self-Actualization:
A New Focus for Education

Our society now calls for each person to achieve a kind of maturity and depth of understanding that is not commonly achieved—self-actualization. Facilitating self-actualization in pupils is a task of the schools through curriculum content and teacher-pupil relations. In order to accomplish this, creative planning for educational reconstruction is imperative.

We can make possible "fulfillment" education for all pupils. While a curriculum revolution may be under way in mathematics and science, one of the most significant human needs has been neglected or overlooked. This need is related to self and the human condition. Only when this need occupies a central position in the curriculum will fulfillment education become a reality. To achieve this kind of education, pupils must come to explore and learn independently. Equally important, they must be introduced to ethics and values.

Specifically, these new directions in education must occur for pupils to become self-actualizing persons.

1. Pupils must select areas of learning or problems which are significant to them.

2. *Pupils must learn how to think creatively and flexibly.*

3. *Pupils must learn to generalize from data and to group ideas in meaningful clusters, if they are to solve problems.*

4. *Pupils must be taught to generate models and theories to explain phenomena.*

5. *Pupils must learn ways to test hypotheses and make critical judgments.*

6. *Pupils, at some point, must arrive at a decision and take a stand.*

5

Self-Actualization: A New Focus for Education

Elizabeth Monroe Drews

    MAN'S quest for meaning is as old as human history.[1] This quest is also—in all healthy, growing individuals—as inevitable as tomorrow. Today's young person is no exception. Yet the modern world with its rapid change and unending alternatives coupled with the disappearance of many conventional guidelines and traditions is not easy to understand and does not serve to reduce the chaos and the fragmentation that many young people experience in the course of living and learning. Innovations in living patterns and new careers (59) appear daily, changes in and additions to knowledge continually accelerate, and out of this maze the young person is asked to choose the fabric and the style of life that he desires. And he is asked to find himself without counsel as to how this might be done.

    A world that seems to be in a continual state of crisis—the pressures of the cold war, the threats of nuclear destruction, the problems of living with and helping alien peoples—calls for each human being to reach a kind of maturity and a depth of understanding not commonly achieved today. We will refer to this positive growth as self-actualization [2] and

---

    [1] This was the subject of philosophy before it became a science and limited its sphere to observed facts and the findings that could be rigorously deduced from these facts.

    [2] The rare individuals whom Maslow feels are self-actualizing have been described as being creative in all of the generally acknowledged ways, as well as being, ". . . altruistic, dedicated, self-transcending, [and] social" (40).

take the stand, in this chapter, that fostering this in all young people will be a vital and rewarding enterprise and well worth the effort entailed. At present there are few attempts to develop programs to help young people achieve self-identity and to experience a sense of universality—of being in communion with other people and with the universe at large. The situation demands, the most thoughtful adults and students agree, that education no longer neglect helping each child enhance his understanding of himself and of others.

This chapter is concerned with suggesting a new direction in education in order directly and intelligently to foster creativity and psychological health in all children. Illustrations will be largely drawn from research conducted with adolescents. Since members of this group, more than any other, face an identity crisis, it seems logical that they be used to illustrate need and readiness for this new focus in education.[3]

For over a decade able students from twelve to eighteen have indicated that they would—if given an opportunity—like very much to have philosophy seminars. In addition, they want opportunities to be independent and they specify a desire to do creative work and research. Most important, they want more time to read, to explore their self dimensions and to discover what the world is all about. However, the typical secondary school rarely is able to offer such freedom or such opportunities for self exploration, and the popular press, neglecting such positive signs, often brands youth as apathetic and alienated.

The students themselves indicate that there may be other problems. Statements which follow were taken from student surveys and indicate the kinds of reactions many of the better students have to routine assignments, competitive grading, memorization and other common school practices.[4]

Classes are filled with busywork. . . .

I don't get a chance to really think. . . . I keep on reading textbooks and making out class schedules, but I don't have time to find out what I like or what I want.

We have to take courses but we're not told why or what their value is.

Assignments and homework keep me from reading and thinking.

[3] There are other considerations in giving emphasis to the adolescent, his needs and talents. The research on growth, including that concerned with affective and cognitive processes, has been mainly with the young—the earlier and simpler manifestations. Sanford, among others, has noted, "Youth is a neglected area as compared with childhood and old age. It is not so much behavior of youth as development in youth that has been neglected" (51).

[4] It should be noted that these comments were made by students who usually do their work and receive relatively good grades but the evidence is that they do not feel that much of what they are asked to do is meaningful.

Sometimes I feel like a memorizing machine. . . . We do not discuss what we learn, we just learn.

Grades become the goal of education. There must be some other reason to study.

Students want school to offer more than it does and they want it to be more relevant to the world in which they live. They are aware of the rapidly changing face and the multi-dimensionality of this world. Many have a spatial orientation and a time perspective far more realistic than do the adults who were born two or three decades before. Knowledge is accelerating, the world is smaller and children undoubtedly have a great deal of talent for dealing with such complexities. Young people read better and more than they ever have and they move into higher level mathematics much sooner than they once did.[5] It is predicted, by the more visionary of the social philosophers (11; 32; 39) that the new human advances will not only embrace such cognitive changes but will also constitute a breakthrough in the realm of moral and spiritual growth. As Maslow says, "A new vision is emerging of the possibilities of man and his destiny" (41).

We hold that the realization of this vision depends, at least partially, on each young person finding his own identity—his own mind and his own will—in a synergic relationship with his society. "What is a good life?" and "How can I find my way?" cannot remain academic questions or the quest of the privileged few. If we have the courage of our conviction that this is the most fundamental need in education today, then we must search for ways to accomplish this goal.

Industrial wealth in Western society now makes it possible for a large proportion of the world's inhabitants to move toward what Aldous Huxley called "full humanity" (30). We are capable, economically, of creating something far better than that which now exists in curriculum and guidance offerings. The scholarly journals contain many suggestions as to how such change might come about. The most farsighted philosophers and social scientists have formulated viable patterns (or workable utopias) which should help people to live together harmoniously and creatively and to work toward both an individual and a social morality (10).

These suggestions for positive social change[6] are coming from many

[5] However, values to live by, a sense of self, and a comprehensive world view (not just a knowledge of bits and pieces) are probably harder to achieve today than ever before.

[6] Always, in addition to these optimistic statements about the future, there are a comparable number of pessimistic statements such as the one credited to an anthropologist: "Ours is the first society that has ever passed from barbarism into decadence without first going through a stage of civilization."

disciplines but tend to be made by the generalists rather than the discipline specialists. The psychologist, Gardner, speaks of the self-renewing individual and the self-renewing society (27) and seems to share many ideas for making the necessary consciously-wrought improvements with his fellow psychologist, Maslow, who sketches in the essentials for eupsychian growth (38). The economist and management specialist, Drucker, holds that these new patterns of education, which he contends that the public is demanding, ". . . will be concerned with basic values —moral, aesthetic, and philosophical" (17). In the same vein, but with a focus on society, the economist, Theobald, outlines the needs of tomorrow's world and states optimistically that we can create ". . . a culture far above anything that existed in the past" (55). Reiser, a philosopher, is also concerned about the society and cautions that we must set our sights high. He contends that we should aim for nothing less than a "fulfillment" society, that the "welfare state" is no longer an adequate goal (48). This might be seen as parallel to helping children respond "creatively" rather than accepting "coping" as an adequate response.

Margaret Mead calls for "conscious creation of conditions within which clusters of evolutionary significance may occur" (42). The Jesuit anthropologist, Teilhard de Chardin, in a similarly utopian formulation, speaks of the possibility of universal man—a creature who has evolved in certain ethical and spiritual ways far above the present level of human development (12). Two biologists express similar views. Julian Huxley has long discussed planned change and speaks hopefully of positive evolution, which he refers to as ". . . a progressive realization of intrinsic possibilities" (31). René Dubos feels that there is no alternative but that the individual with his new power to change the universe will assume a more responsible attitude toward himself and toward the universe he inhabits. Dubos sees these ". . . powers of action [as] so great that the classical discussions of the good life now take on very practical meaning" (18).

We are suggesting that creative planning for educational reconstruction is an imperative. Our belief is that we must devise and make possible "fulfillment" education. The idea is not as radical or as impractical as it sounds. Many educators have already recognized and responded to the situation. A curriculum revolution, focused particularly on mathematics and science teaching, is under way (28). In these fields the effort is to match what is taught to the young with current knowledge. And yet, one of the most significant human needs and a subject which has been carefully (if not conclusively) studied—the self and the human condition—is still neglected. Students are not introduced to possibilities of moral and intellectual change and they are not given models to help them in shaping their own life styles. However, this does not mean that educators are unconcerned.[7]

The membership of the Association for Supervision and Curriculum Development has shown a strong inclination to accept the ideal of self-actualization as a basic goal in education. The ASCD 1962 Yearbook, which dealt with perceiving, behaving and becoming, was read eagerly and was widely discussed (3). Most ASCD members would probably agree with Maslow that there is much talent that never flowers and that, all too frequently, a large majority who could become self-actualizing persons do not. Yet, more hopefully, there was recognition in this volume, and I am sure by the ASCD membership, that children have great (but untapped) talent for creative growth. Thus we may conclude that while most of us hold self-development to be a major educational goal and decry the apathy of youth, today's schools, if we can accept a review of the professional literature as evidence, are doing little to change the situation. Few of the efforts in curriculum change focus on self-actualization; and "fulfillment" counseling is practically unknown. Guidance clinics and mental health facilities do not concern themselves with fostering psychological health through carefully planned educational programs. Instead, psychotherapy remains largely remedial and rarely becomes a venture in self-actualization. What is lacking is a program or a variety of programs to help young people dedicate themselves to those things worth living for.

A program for self-actualization must foster motivation to think—creatively and critically about self and the world; and it must provide materials and aids for the teacher—program guides and directives. If we plan to identify and foster creative attitudes and to help students convert these into constructive behavior, such steps must be taken. We have some knowledge as to how this may be done. For example, suggestions as to ways to plan and put into effect a more creative education can be derived from the experiences of many who work with young people.[8] These ideas must then be unified with the most current findings in sociology, psychology, educational methods and counseling. Thoughtful

---

[7] There is a great deal of evidence of the extensive scholarship in this area. Note particularly the work which has been done in personalist philosophy by men such as Martin Buber. There is not only much talk about the "I-thou" relationship, commitment and intersubjectivity in philosophy, but the psychologists who study the self carry on a similar dialogue as can be seen in the writings of Bühler, Combs, Fromm, May, Maslow, Rogers, Snygg and others.

[8] This includes a variety of youth workers and counselors as well as teachers.

consideration of such proposals could provide a wealth of workable plans for this new focus in education.

Undoubtedly vast amounts of theory building and research are needed if we are to understand human learning, motivation and values, but our point is that we do have many insights and theories that have not been put into practice. Only by such actions can we accomplish the purpose of education—which is, as Kant saw it, not just to prepare youth for the present, but to create a better society.

Both education and society must begin more effectively to serve all children and youth. Programs must be vastly more differentiated to meet the needs and abilities of a great range of young human beings. For example, the junior high schools contain many children who do not read at all (and seemingly have no appetite for the undertaking) and others who comprehend difficult treatises at the college graduate level (and have a voracious hunger for all forms of the printed word). In addition, content must be expanded and methods revised if education is to make sense in a modern world. Methods and materials in general use today, and which generally do not take into account this great range of individual differences, mitigate against optimum school learning by the child and do not prepare him to take responsibility for his own life and his own future in an open and dynamic society.[9] We have not begun to develop human learning capacity or to cultivate the fresh and open curiosity needed if intellectual and emotional growth are to continue.

Although educational psychologists recognize that personality development must parallel cognitive development, there is little effort to build school programs (especially at the secondary level) in which a balanced affective and intellectual growth is encouraged. Children must learn how to explore and discover and learn independently and they must become aware of the kaleidoscopic qualities and multiplicity of the worlds in which they live. Beyond this, they must be introduced to ethics and values and, of course, the human condition. New approaches are being explored by the academic community and by public school people which could be used to help the young person think, creatively and responsibly, about his life—and the world in which he lives. It is our

---

[9] Good teachers as well as the better students are finding the use of a single, fixed-content hard-cover textbook inappropriate to meet the needs of the range of abilities and learning styles in the typical classroom. Similarly, there is increasing recognition that page-to-page reading assignments do not foster critical and creative thinking. A student who was exposed to an open-ended course with a flexible textbook had this to say, "It's so encouraging to get away from the grind of schoolbooks. In this class I can study and work by myself and not be bothered with the usual kind of homework as in other classes."

opinion that such "fulfillment" education must be offered if the human being is to continue to evolve and if the self-actualizing individual is to become more than a rare accident.

Of course this new vision of education is not wholly *new* or utterly unprecedented. As we have seen, the quest for meaning and self-understanding (the ideal of the fullest possible development) is an ancient one. Similarly it has long been held that this is the essence of and the *raison d'être* for a liberal education. What would be new is that concentrated and thoughtful effort would be exerted by large numbers of educators to bring such dreams into realization.

Innovations of this order in the school program would bring into being many other changes. Schools would have to make room in their schedules for students to devote time to this new subject, the self, and the universities would have to prepare teachers and counselors to relate to these problems and to students as they seek to answer such questions as "Who am I?" and "What might I become?" All academic subjects could be applied in this new context. Knowledge could be seen as meaningful in terms of the developing self. Education would exhibit not just a belief that existing reality could be understood, but that each individual could be effective in bringing into being a potential reality.

In attempting to introduce a new emphasis in education, we must not, of course, violate what we know about the child and youth,[10] although there will necessarily be new content, new methods, extrapolations beyond our present technology and efforts to transcend what is today the usual classroom situation. It is observed, "The brush in the hand of the artist becomes the extension of the hand." In short, the emphasis must be on acting not only in terms of what is probable (if existing trends continue) but what is possible (if education will take seriously the directive of helping the individual to become self-actualized). Our belief is that we should not be overly impressed with the past and that we can and must, in truth, influence the future. As Anne Roe has said, "We must keep the inevitable from happening" (49).

The reader may at this point protest and suggest that we are going too far, that we should be content to do well what we are doing now. We have thought about this and rejected this course as too limited an objective. If, as Francois Bloch-Lainé says, one does not attempt a very great deal, one never attains as much as might be possible (5). These

[10] Not all of this knowledge is (or ever will be) in neat statistical tables—much of it will always be inchoate and incomplete. Thus we must use intuitional guesses along with the hard facts as we plan to bring about a future which, as yet, we can barely imagine but which is seemingly endless and has almost unlimited possibilities.

ideal purposes are not unlike those of democracy itself (this was the first universal and secular utopia) and our task is to translate the American Dream which pervades our educational theory into meaningful action. Thus we are suggesting an education for self-actualization and competency which deals with self as content and makes a concerted effort to teach children to think and to care.

An Experimental Program

The suggested directions for education and considerations about youth which we must keep in mind may sound much too large and too complex for thinking about, much less taking action on. However, *these are the problems and the needs* and—with the quality of life or life itself at stake—we should not equivocate. One may ask whether we have evidence that such a program will be successful. Although we admit that our own efforts to work on the problem can still only be classed as "trial" or "pilot," we believe we have clues as to how to proceed.

Our study was concerned with testing a new program designed to foster self-initiated learning and psychological maturity. Using 250 college-bound ninth-graders (randomly placed in experimental and control groups, one group of each in four junior high schools), we found that we were able to engage students in discussions relating to crucial issues in the world, to the human condition and to the self. Focus was provided by a flexible book (entitled the *Four Worlds Textbook*) and by ten style-of-life films of creative, intellectually alive, and socially concerned men and women, the *Being and Becoming Film Series*.

Our effort in this research was to introduce the construct of self-actualization and at the same time to have students engage in study of self in relation to the larger world. We reasoned that by observing and studying a number of self-actualized role models [11] (shown in documentary-biographical films, or by their writings and biographies), the students would begin to form a clear and conscious concept of self-actualizing behavior and would see this behavior as both personally rewarding and socially desirable. Assessment instruments chosen were ones that had successfully discriminated, in terms of attitudes, values and interests,

---

[11] These individuals were chosen on the basis of the descriptions worked out by psychologists [such as MacKinnon (35)] who have described the creative adult and Maslow's descriptions of the self-actualizing individual (37). They were selected for demonstrated excellence in intellectual and creative behaviors and highly developed social consciences. The eight style-of-life films portray: Eugene Petersen, historian; Mary Coleman, judge; Robert von Neumann, artist; Barbara Radmore, radiologist; Kay Britten, singer; Loren Eiseley, natural scientist; Anne Roe, social scientist; and Harold Taylor, philosopher.

creative adults and college students from less creative ones. These included the *Omnibus Personality Inventory*, the Allport-Vernon-Lindzey *Study of Values* and the ACE *Critical Thinking Test, Form G.*

Results on a number of scales showed that our pilot program was effective at least to the extent that the experimental students rated significantly higher than controls at post-testing on the indicated instruments as well as on several informal scales which the investigator had developed. The measures were designed to assess motivation to learn, openness to psychological growth and humanitarian-altruistic values. The experimental boys' self-image changed toward significantly more choices at post-testing of a self-description designated as "creative intellectual" than was true of control boys. The experimental girls also held a different self-image at the end of the program than did the control group. For example, 62 percent of the experimental girls chose as their ideal self description a statement which emphasized self-actualization, whereas only 31 percent of the control girls chose this self-image.

Scales which distinguished experimental students from the controls at the end of the program included those testing theoretical orientation and aesthetic orientation, thinking introversion (philosophical orientation), originality, and humanitarian-altruistic attitudes.[12] Experimentals also tested significantly higher on critical thinking and chose more "creative intellectual" activities in school and more "creative intellectual" reasons for occupational choice. In addition, experimental girls rated significantly higher on an instrument, entitled *Acceptance of Women Scale,* designed to show an acceptance of women committed to creative, high level service or career roles.

Can such a program be used in other situations, for other grade levels, for below average students as well as for those who are above average? We think it can. Our survey of psychological literature unearthed a good deal of supporting experimental evidence which comes from studies which have attempted to change other characteristics. In addition, program development efforts [13] with the lower third of the school population have shown that these students, too, respond extremely well to special approaches and materials that are less school-like and more relevant to life. In one experiment (14), four groups of slow learners who had spent a year in a specially designed program and in small, relatively homogeneous class groups, where the emphasis was on

[12] Aesthetic orientation and humanitarian-altruistic attitudes were significantly different only for the experimental girls in comparison with the control girls.

[13] In which the writer has been involved over the past two decades and which first were concerned with understanding and teaching slow learners and students with reading disabilities.

reading and discussion, became much more self-confident and more interested in school than an equivalent group of slow learners who remained in regular English classes. These slower students particularly liked to talk about themselves and their immediate problems. When asked to evaluate the program, these students did not mention academic learning but, instead, stressed that they had found friends, an accepting teacher and a new confidence in themselves. It is our conclusion that if reading abilities, the style or level of thinking, and the interests of pupils are kept in mind, programs can be developed which will make a great deal of difference in the personal growth of the individual.

From the literature, from our earlier research and from our work with the able young people in the experiment which used the *Four Worlds Textbook* and the *Being and Becoming Film Series*, we have drawn up certain principles which we believe are appropriate for developing curriculum and guidance innovations. We believe that these principles may serve as guides when the effort is to contribute to self-actualizing attitudes and behaviors in young people. We are convinced that a carefully planned program based on such principles can make a great deal of difference as to how young people feel about themselves and about school.

Propositions About Youth and About Education

The propositions which follow, first a set of eight dealing with the characteristics of youth and then three detailing new directions in education, have evolved out of all these influences. Assumptions about the individual and his development that seem both valid and relevant for a program which focuses on self-actualization follow:

1. Each individual is different from every other one and these differences are desirable and should be fostered. Differences increase with more education and as students get older. The longer the educational process (e.g., the optimum would be lifelong education [14])—if the student takes responsibility for his own learning—the richer and more productive his life will be.

2. Each individual has potential which is not used; in fact, the mind has unfathomed possibilities and the limits of human potentiality are still unknown.

[14] Every young person must understand that his education has to be continuous and lifelong. Several years ago Oppenheimer remarked, "Nearly everything that is now known was not in any book when most of us went to school; we cannot know it unless we have picked it up since" (47). Similarly, the scientist-philosopher, Dubos, has recently pointed out, "In many fields, the wisdom of the father is no longer of use to the son" (19).

3. Abilities must be developed and used if the individual is to be psychologically healthy. In other words, as an individual becomes self-actualized, his mental health increases.

4. In the development of attitudes and abilities, interaction will always be between organism and environment, though each individual must develop according to his own design.

5. Each individual seeks to learn about himself and others in the course of his development, although this search may not always be a conscious one.

6. The more highly developed individuals are characterized by a high degree of differentiation (complexity) and a high degree of integration (wholeness). In spite of this diversity of characteristics, all self-actualized individuals have certain qualities in common: a fundamental stability (i.e., developed values), a sense of direction and purpose, an independence of thought and action, a capacity to carry out commitments to self and others, an openness to new experience (a capacity to be alive and aware), a richness of imagination, and a motivation to learn.

7. The individual is all of a piece and functions as a unit. Intellect, feeling, emotion and action can be separated conceptually yet no one of these functions independently of the others.

8. The values and purposes of the individual (the development of character) are central to education. Nothing is learned until it is integrated with the purposes of the individual.

Our studies have not only led us to accept these propositions about the needs of youth but have also convinced us that educational innovations are particularly needed in the social studies-humanities area. As we mentioned before, we realized that our own efforts to develop a new program would be exploratory and tentative, but we also came to believe that there was no alternative but to make the effort. Our conclusions have been that there is a vital need to demonstrate and help young people find more democratic and humane ways of living. We suspect that many of the present patterns of education do not do this. Education which conditions children to repeat textbook formulas and unquestioningly to accept teacher dictum, which concentrates on the problems of the past and teaching children as if they were all alike, obviously, does not prepare young people to become self-actualizing. And it does not prepare them to live in today's society. The changes we suggest will entail re-thinking every aspect of the educational program and will involve helping both the teachers and young people understand what this different kind of education is all about.

We felt that both teachers and students would come to care more about education if they were directly involved in the program change themselves (they helped, in our program, to make the flexible textbook and served as consultants to the film-maker). It is our conviction that changes can be made which will increase motivation to learn and cultivate an openness of mind and heart—both necessary for self-actualization. Such a reconstruction of education will be most apt to occur:

1. If education is redefined and students accept its new meaning
2. If new skills and ways of learning are taught, and
3. If curriculum content is revised.

These approaches are held to be fundamental if the aim of education is to teach young people to think critically and creatively about themselves and their society. Each point is discussed more fully in the following section.

New Directions in Education

Education Redefined

The considerations discussed in the preceding pages have led us strongly to recommend an education which has a new emphasis—self-actualization. This will not be an easy task for it will demand, to a considerable extent, a redefinition of education. If students are to develop their intellectual and creative potential (2), they must have a vision of what they might become, they must learn to live examined lives and begin to search for a life philosophy. And each will have to become responsible for his own education. Students who have had opportunities to search for a life philosophy and to take responsibility for their own education have responded favorably.[15] One who had spent a half year in such a program remarked, "It has helped me to understand the problems of the world and where I fit in to help solve them. It seems as though my eyes have been opened."

We believe that education must be redefined for many students, and sometimes for their teachers as well, if the students are to assume responsibility for their own education. Students often feel they are "being educated" by outer forces, that an education is something that happens to a person, but they do not understand that they can make it happen or how they can make it happen. We must ask several questions:

How can we help students to think creatively about their own lives?

---

[15] All students' comments are verbatim statements made by college-bound ninth graders involved in a semester's program (five classes a week) planned to foster self discovery, independent learning, and self-actualization.

How can we help students become more fully aware of themselves and of how they feel?

How can we help students become more independent in their efforts to learn?

How can we help students work toward developing a unifying philosophy of education and of life?

The task of attempting to answer these questions and solve these problems is of central importance to each child and to all teachers; but the answers do not come easily. We must enlarge our understandings of self psychology and the construct of self-actualization; we must try to understand the learning process better than is now the case; we must do more than give lip service to teaching children to think; and we must prepare new material—attractive in format and significant in content—for these tasks. The learning environment must become more responsive and evocative than it has been in the past and teachers must become more skilled as counselors and consultants.

If we are serious about producing changes in this direction, one of the most effective means will be to help the student understand and accept the objective of self-actualization. He must realize that the point of his education is personal growth—intellectual, emotional and moral. To the extent that this becomes a key motivating force in his life, he will be apt to move in that direction and, because he rehearses the ideas frequently, his learning will be more lasting and meaningful. Students seem to come to this viewpoint readily. As one said:

The people in the (*Being and Becoming*) films are still learning, aren't they? I used to think that when you memorized your schoolwork, that was all you had to know, but these people are still trying to learn something new all the time.

We are suggesting that the concept of self-actualization must become a clear and conscious one for the students and for teachers as well. The very act of conceptualizing the idea will lead to a more complete and a higher level of understanding.

In accepting such a direction of development as being possible, we agree with Julian Huxley: "The next decisive step in evolution will . . . be the fuller development of self-consciousness" (33). This parallels the more optimistic view of man taken by the "third force" psychologists.[16] For example, Allport, in discussing the forward thrust of "becoming," sees man not only as a "self-conscious" but also as a rational creature who creates his own style and his own future (1). The consensus is that, given a healthy organism and a responsive environment, the direction of growth and the choice made will probably be good.

---

[16] Among the "third force" psychologists are G. Allport, C. Bühler, E. Fromm, K. Goldstein, R. May, A. Maslow, G. Murphy, C. Rogers and H. Sullivan.

The student who is seeking an identity must clearly understand that this process cannot be one of simply confirming himself as he is; rather the process must be one of attempting to become all that he can be. In addition, students will need to understand that education continues throughout life and is integral with all aspects of living. For this to happen, the student should not only be conscious of the need to grow but he also must begin to reach out into the surrounding world and begin to discover various life styles. Gradually, he will come to unite these new ideas with his existing images. Class discussions, led by an empathic, warm and self-revealing teacher will help this to happen (50). There seems little doubt that students will take such self-revelations seriously and become deeply involved. After many discussions centering on life philosophy, one student commented:

> Class discussions helped me to understand that people are not machines. They are really living creatures with many variable feelings and interests. Before this class was open to me, I always thought a person was just the kid next door or my teacher, but now I know more about the deep person behind this face.

If we want to help a student become responsible for his own education, we must make it clear to him that we consider this to be his task and are willing to make it possible. We must define learning in these terms, telling students they can, of their own volition, change, improve and become educated. After a semester of reviewing world issues and contemplating life styles, another student commented:

> The understanding of myself has increased greater than anything else. No other class has even considered the individual important. I think this class shed light on that for most of us.

Demonstrating—through models or films—how others come to understand themselves and take responsibility for their lives can be particularly helpful. Of course, there must be leeway (saying, in effect, there are many ways—choose one that suits you), and time (hours and days, not minutes), as well as materials that have built-in flexibility and by their very nature ask for individual adaptations and innovations. None of this can be forced. There must be only the suggestions, the models, and the opportunities for self-direction. Sometimes even the shy will respond as did one very quiet boy who concluded, "What better way is there for you to look at yourself than by bringing yourself out from hiding?"

Forcing students to be independent is neither appropriate nor effective (although mother robins do push their young out of the nest). We feel it is best, instead, to suggest and if the student is fearful and unready, he can, in effect, say, "I will not be responsible. I will learn only what I am told." However, students who are intellectually able and psychologically healthy take to responsibility and independence readily. One boy remarked:

> This course has stimulated me into finding hundreds of things I never realized or even had the slightest inkling of. I never knew that deep philosophical theories could be so interesting and captivating. Many things like, Education; God and Evolution; Humanity.

Such students have not been reduced to passive dependency. Our surveys have repeatedly shown that superior students generally choose as an ideal self an image or description which approaches self-actualization, although they may feel in reality that they fall short of the mark.

In the broadest sense, to be educated is to learn to live. Although students may only vaguely understand learning as a lifetime task, all students can come to see their education as a full-time endeavor which consumes every waking hour. Students must see that there are many intellectual and creative pursuits (non-symbolic as well as symbolic, humanistic as well as scientific) in which they might engage and which will make a difference both to the student and to the world in which he or she lives. One girl said, after reading the *Four Worlds Textbook:*

> I have been reading so many new things, about different aspects of the world and all the problems that exist. Even though I'm a little thing in a great world, I can contribute by just trying.

Education and knowledge should become open systems with the student continually learning to deal with more of himself and more of reality. As Margaret Mead says, this can result in ". . . an enlargement of the stage on which every individual acts" (43). To participate fully in education, students must learn the art of adequate experiencing and be given training in perceiving and imagining. School and learning can be an illuminating and entertaining experience or a dull and pedantic one. To augment awareness and social participation, we must, as Ojemann has shown, help each student not only to take responsibility for his own development but to comprehend the dynamics of his behavior as well (45). Such understandings will counteract present-day tendencies to abstract cognition and learning from their living context. Learning must never be seen—by the student, the teacher or the researcher—as independent from the learner or from the total environment in which he lives.

New Skills and New Approaches to Learning

If we accept as a thesis that democratic and mutually supportive ways of living together are good ways, we must realize that we endorse hope. As Gardner says, ". . . democracy demands a certain optimism concerning mankind" (25). This optimism is even more apparent if we endorse self-actualization as an appropriate and necessary educational goal. The concept of helping young people to become self-conscious, rational beings who create their own style and their own future is utopian in the most modern and idealistic interpretation of the word. This view sees youth as "effective" not merely reactive, as responding creatively not simply coping, and as planning rather than just managing.

Thus creative problem solving, as Dewey has pointed out, is not only the common denominator of the scientific method but also the method of political democracy (13). However, a sense of personal effectiveness and the development of talent in creative and critical thinking skills usually do not occur spontaneously or by accident. By one means or another, and to the extent that the talent is mastered, people learn to think. Our thesis is that *young people can be taught to think* but we are forced to agree with some of the children who comment, "People say thinking is a good thing—especially for children. But they don't tell us how and they don't give us anything very important to think about."

Fortunately a few research workers have taken these directives seriously. Bruner has explored problem solving—particularly discovery methods—in *The Process of Education* (9) and, more recently, has looked at the more subjective aspects of the process in *On Knowing: Essays for the Left Hand* (8). Gallagher has reviewed current research in what is called "productive thought" (24) and both he and Guilford (29) have studied certain aspects of creative thinking in the classroom. Torrance also has explored this area and developed and tried out imaginative ways for teaching school children to think creatively (58). Taba has done a long term and carefully thought-through study concerned with teaching children to think in the social studies area (54). Suchman has developed ingenious approaches to group and individual problem solving called "inquiry process" (52) and the science and mathematics research and curriculum teams have made great progress in rewriting curriculum materials in these areas and incorporating problem solving and scientific thinking into programs of study (34).

Learning to think and to learn are crucial to the process of self-discovery. A sense of identity and "full humanity" can only come when students have learned to collect a wide range of information, to evaluate it carefully and to make wise decisions. As Tillich has noted, a man is never more human than at the moment of decision (57). However it is our contention that many students (including many who have high intellectual potential) will not maintain an eagerness to learn and a willingness to think if there is no opportunity for them to practice thinking and problem solving in school. Without opportunities to make discoveries and choices in terms of their own thoughts and wishes—to fulfill their humanity through moments of decision—students will find it difficult to discover themselves. In other words, the exercise of choice is an affirmation of selfhood.

Talent in managing reality without (the outer world) and within (the inner world) will increase as students learn to take responsibility for their education. It will improve both because students practice these skills and because each act of independent discovery (about themselves and the world) will give them a sense of power. Engagement in thinking (rather than merely memorizing) will also allow students, as Dewey suggested, to internalize their learnings. Such processes—discovering on one's own and putting ideas into one's own words—will also enhance the storage and retrieval of ideas.

In building a program that will foster critical thinking, ample opportunity should be given for students to "try out" ideas, add new insights, and make their own decisions. We also felt it was necessary that each student understand that such independent learning and problem solving was important, and also that he understand why it was important. Some of the major propositions to be kept in mind and communicated to the students follow:

Students must choose areas of learning or problems which appeal to them. They will learn best if there is a "thorn in the flesh" (Northrup's term for materials which rankle and then instigate thought) and if they really want to know something. If vital and controversial issues and a wide range of possibilities and alternatives are presented, students are apt to find problems that appeal or they may, perhaps, fashion a new problem.

When introduced to new possibilities and given opportunity to make choices one student said:

There were many things I found interesting I probably never would have discovered on my own. Art and music were much more interesting and alive than I thought they would be. I learned I got more out of the *Saturday Review* than *Motor Trend.*

Students must learn how to think flexibly and creatively. Ideatracking and brainstorming in free-form group discussions can help each student go far beyond the limits of his usual perceptions and understandings. Oral expression of thoughts may also lead to "Inner Dialogue," which Jung considered an imperative for self-discovery. We believe that the classroom should provide many opportunities for such oral discourse and dialogue in a non-judgmental atmosphere and in open unstructured situations. What we have termed "the conversational dialectic" could provide opportunities for exchange and paraphrase that would directly enrich the student's symbolic skills. Other kinds of discovery can come from the openness discussed earlier (see "Education Redefined") which flexible materials and an accepting teacher will encourage. Beyond choosing an area for study and finding how best to express himself in talking with others, the students should be taught how to search in wide-ranging ways.

If they are to solve problems, students must learn to generalize from data and to group ideas in meaningful clusters. If the student learns to search he will also begin to ask questions. If the classroom climate is accepting and the teaching and materials are evocative, students should produce a large number of viable hypotheses and theories. Teachers can, by example, show how this is done. We believe that, by presenting important issues as well as an array of solutions and certain unifying principles, students can be helped to choose, to try out, and to form more intelligent hypotheses. It is important to remember that in teaching critical thinking there should be a warm and accepting classroom climate. Students will need to feel accepted as well as challenged. Further, speculation, search and discovery will probably not occur if the teacher insists that there is only one way to do a problem or one right answer and will not tolerate the educated guess.

One student recalled this incident from his experience in the eighth grade:

Last year in a science course, I couldn't work out one of the problems in the way the teacher showed us. I thought a lot about it, and got the answer in an entirely different way, but the teacher wouldn't accept it. She said it wasn't right because I hadn't done it the way the book said.

Students must be taught to form ideas and images of what might be; they must generate models and theories to explain phenomena. This will mean that teachers will use models, theories and generalizations and that they must characteristically "lift" thinking by showing students how to draw relationships, parallels and analogies between seemingly unrelated events. Such common components are essential aspects of theory building. Teachers must be able to help students use techniques that bring together (in probable relationships) an array of diverse phenomena. Thus students can come to see that fragments (what appears to be unrelated knowledge) can be related, unified and explained—and often in one or more alternative ways. Such efforts on the part of the teacher do not go unnoticed by the students. One student commented:

This is my first experience with a teacher who helps us when we want to deal with "important" issues, like "Whither Mankind?" I guess a teacher needs to be pretty special to be interested in what we think when we're in ninth grade and to help us think problems through.

Students must learn ways to test hypotheses and to make critical judgments. An attitude of optimistic skepticism is basic to problem solving—the student must feel that answers are available but that each is to be tested against logic and information. If materials on key issues which students read contain several alternatives and these are vividly and cogently stated, students may come, by comparing possibilities, to recognize shallow reasoning and *non sequitur* conclusions. In an open forum with intelligent teacher leadership, they may recognize distorted and incompatible statements and pointless questions. As one student said, "Before, I often reached a conclusion by emotion rather than reasoning. But now it's the other way around." We believe that this will happen if we present examples of adults who are thinking critically. We also believe that teachers can make a contribution by setting the stage for discussions and by helping each one to understand that other students could disagree with his ideas while respecting him as an individual.

Students must finally realize that at some point they will have to make a decision and take a stand. They must see that making choices is a skill which goes beyond tracing, relating and evaluating, to a realization that the attitudes and actions of each individual are vital forces in the lives of others. It is at this point that the student may learn the meaning of responsibility.

We feel that students can best learn to take a stand and make a responsible choice by coming to know that adults who are influential in our society, teachers included, think things through, make decisions carefully and have ethical concerns about the consequences of their decisions. They will, of course, find that many adults and many of their student friends do not seem to make either ethical or logical decisions, that they do not characteristically examine the assumptions they hold or do not regularly check for bias and prejudice before they make a statement. Free discussion can make a difference particularly when there are two-way conversations and students and teachers listen to one another. The student's conscience becomes enlightened and stabilized through confrontation (discussion). One student summarized her feelings as follows:

> When a teacher talks with you, not at you, he really seems to care about you and not just that you memorize his lessons. When he really listens to what you say, it makes you feel like you are accomplishing something. You feel like a real person.

There are, of course, many ways in which a student can develop intellectually, search for truth and solve problems. Many definitions and specified steps have been given for such activities as scientific thinking, creative thinking, and critical thinking. No effort to generalize can cover all possibilities; neither can we even predict the order in which any given individual will proceed. A teacher will often understand how a given student thinks if there are frequent class discussions which meet some of the requirements of critical and creative thinking. These may be structured in the manner similar to the "20 questions" approach, which Suchman used in inquiry training (53), the Socratic method, which Oliver used in teaching social studies (46); or quite unstructured as in the free discussions in our experimental program and which we have called the "conversational dialectic" (15). In all of these approaches, the important thing to remember is that action and personal involvement on the part of the student contribute to learning and change (4).

New Content and Materials

If we take our stated purpose seriously, i.e., if we want students to become self-actualized—to experience themselves as worthwhile and unique individuals who at the same time have a sense of shared purposes with others—we must change the materials in the curriculum. Gardner puts it this way:

> If we believe what we profess concerning the worth of the individual, then the idea of individual fulfillment within a framework of moral purpose must become our deepest concern, our national preoccupation, our passion, our obsession (26).

We know that young people are, to a very large extent, what they experience. If we want them to develop a sense of integrity and a social conscience, they should be exposed to individuals who exemplify these qualities and to materials that present important theories or philosophies of a humane and social nature. A student who had been reading widely on world issues and in biographies commented, "Albert Schweitzer's reverence for life made the biggest impression on me. He always loved his fellow man and helped him whenever he could." This may serve, in some measure, to balance the daily diet of scandal, sex and crime which mass media offer. Special materials will have to be prepared, since, as Robert White says,

> ... [there are] scarcely any systematic case records of great fortitude, rare heroism, unusual contribution to the arts or special success with grasping and solving important social issues. The natural growth of personality and the higher flights of human achievement have been given almost no representation in man's current ideas of himself (60).

Young people will not be able to redefine education and learn new skills and approaches unless the content and the means by which this content is presented are changed in dramatic ways. For a decade the "curriculum revolution" has been under way but it is only now beginning to touch social studies and the humanities. With appropriate materials in these areas, students will not only develop an adequate grasp of the intellectual disciplines, but they will be more apt to develop an adequate conception of knowledge and of self. They will learn the range and possibilities of human excellence if they meet "significant others" and if they are given an opportunity to "stand on the shoulders of giants." In this way, creative expansion may become their modal behavior style, and they may avoid typical student behavior—where answers are given too quickly, knowledge is treated too cursorily, and even careers are chosen hastily and carelessly. Thus, behavior can become self-transcending rather than self-confirming.

We must examine our offerings to students and attempt to fill in the gaps and to supply materials that will be important aids to constructive growth. We can show how man shapes his environment, we can depict human beings with a sense of destiny, rather than focusing, as White says psychology has done, ". . . mainly on man's irrationality and helplessness" (61). Materials that present such ideas and concepts can make a very great difference to a single student or to a group of young people. One student who felt he had changed commented,

> Harold Taylor, the philosopher, is the most interesting person. He broke my idea of a philosopher because he doesn't just think about something, he does something!

As Mumford has said, man is "the unfinished animal," he is influenced by what he sees and hears and reads,

> The final stage of his growth is not determined by his biological past; it rests with himself and is partly determined by his own plans for the future (44).

The individuals whom students meet and the materials that students read should release the young people from the limitations of the classroom and should take them into the artist's studio and the scientist's laboratory and, more important, the young people should come to understand how these individuals think. One student reacted to the style-of-life film of a philosopher-artist:

> Robert von Neumann was an excellent example of the artist who really thinks about his work, likes it, and expresses the thoughts, beauties and actions of nature. He seemed very dedicated—his chosen field was a way of life and he loved it.

Students should also be introduced to kinds of reading, such as magazines of critical commentary and scientific journals, quite unlike "school type" materials.

Adolescents, and especially those who are intellectually superior, are able to think abstractly and reflectively, can deal with important topics and have a concern for what Erikson has called fidelity (21). Teaching materials can be developed with these concepts in mind. Students are aware of the complexity of the modern world, and they know we are living in an era of accelerated change, but we have not given them a metalanguage or metaskills which will allow them to deal with the continuity of change.[17] Although we may not be able to provide all of the needed information, language and skills for dealing with the future, we can show students how others contemplate reorganization (56) or even "invent the future" (23).

For those who are concerned with the personal development of youth, who feel that our existing offerings are not providing adequate intellectual and moral sustenance and who are inclined to do something about the problem, communication research offers some direction. For example, investigations have shown that materials should be believable. In other words, respected sources such as the actual statements of esteemed individuals will carry greater impact than less vividly stated and less valued conclusions (e.g., from a secondary source such as a textbook).[18] A student comment points up this observation,

> It seems to me that President Kennedy was talking directly to me when he said, "Ask not what your country can do for you: Ask what you can do for your

---

[17] Bruner believes that mathematics is the most general of metalanguages, noting that it provides the forms and patterns in terms of which regularities in nature are comprehended. He also feels that poetry performs a similar function in that it helps with the search for likenesses beneath the surface of diversity and change—is a vehicle for searching out unexpected kinship (7).

[18] Students will need to be taught to evaluate sources carefully, as was indicated in the section on "New Skills and New Approaches to Learning." They can, for example, learn to respect research findings more than hearsay.

country." That really inspires me to want to do something useful. I never considered before that one person could make a difference.

Beyond this it is well to keep in mind that students will be more apt to remember and think about ideas if they are given the symbols (words or labels) for doing this thinking. Thoughts, including attitudes such as motivation to learn or to find out, are symbolic acts which are rehearsed often and, if teaching materials are to be effective, should be tied to real acts and are therefore apt to produce behavior changes (6). Such relevance, i.e., materials that strike students as being relevant to a world they know and understand, will be most apt to produce behavior changes and learning.

References

1. Gordon Allport. *Becoming.* New Haven: Yale University Press, 1955.
2. John E. Arnold. "The Generalist Versus the Specialist in Research and Development." *The Creative Person.* The proceedings of a conference held at the Tahoe Alumni Center, October 13-17, 1961; Donald W. MacKinnon, Director. Berkeley: The Institute of Personality Assessment and Research, University of California, 1961.
3. Association for Supervision and Curriculum Development. *Perceiving, Behaving, Becoming: A New Focus for Education,* Yearbook 1962. Washington, D.C.: Association for Supervision and Curriculum Development, 1962.
4. Bernard Berelson and Gary Steiner. *Human Behavior: An Inventory of Scientific Findings.* New York: Harcourt, Brace and World, Inc., 1964.
5. Francois Bloch-Lainé. "The Utility of Utopias for Reformers." *Daedalus* 94 (2): 419-36; Spring 1965.
6. Roger W. Brown. *Words and Things.* New York: Free Press of Glencoe, Inc., 1958.
7. Jerome Bruner. "Education as Social Invention." *The Journal of Social Issues* 20 (3): 21-33; July 1964.
8. Jerome S. Bruner. *On Knowing: Essays for the Left Hand.* Cambridge: The Belknap Press of Harvard University Press, 1962.
9. Jerome S. Bruner. *The Process of Education.* Cambridge: Harvard University Press, 1960.
10. *Daedalus.* "Utopia." Reprinted by permission from *Daedalus,* published by the American Academy of Arts and Sciences, Brookline, Massachusetts, Vol. 94, No. 1, Science and Culture.
11. Teilhard de Chardin. *The Phenomenon of Man.* New York: Harper & Brothers, 1959.
12. *Ibid.*
13. John Dewey. *Democracy in Education.* New York: Macmillan Company, 1916.

14. Elizabeth M. Drews. "The Effect of Homogeneous and Heterogeneous Ability Grouping in Ninth Grade English Classes with Slow, Average and Superior Students." *Student Abilities, Grouping Patterns and Classroom Interaction*. Final Report of the Cooperative Research Program, 608, U.S. Office of Education. East Lansing, Michigan: Office of Research and Publications, College of Education, Michigan State University, 1963.

15. Elizabeth M. Drews. "The Effectiveness of Audio-Visuals in Changing Aspirations of Intellectually Superior Students," Phase I. *The Creative Intellectual Style in Gifted Adolescents*, Being and Becoming: A Cosmic Approach to Counseling and Curriculum. Report II in a series of three: Final Report for the Media Branch, Title VII, N.D.E.A. Contract No. 7-32-0420-140, U.S. Office of Education. East Lansing, Michigan: Office of Research and Publications, College of Education, Michigan State University, 1965.

16. Elizabeth Monroe Drews. "A Study of Non-Intellectual Factors in Superior (Average, and Slow) High School Students." *The Creative Intellectual Style in Gifted Adolescents*, Motivation to Learn: Attitudes, Interests, and Values. Report I in a series of three: Final Report of the Cooperative Research Program, E-2, U.S. Office of Education. East Lansing, Michigan: College of Education, Michigan State University, 1964.

17. Peter F. Drucker. "American Directions: A Forecast." *Harper's Magazine* 230: 39-46; February 1965.

18. René Dubos. "Humanistic Biology." *American Scholar* 34: 179-99; Spring 1965. Copyright © 1965 by the United Chapters of Phi Beta Kappa. By permission of the publishers.

19. René Dubos. "Science and Man's Nature." *Daedalus* 94: 223-45; Winter 1965.

20. Lee Erickson. An unpublished survey of Michigan State University undergraduates.

21. Erik Erikson. "Youth: Fidelity and Diversity." *Daedalus* 91: 5-27; Winter 1962.

22. Edgar Friedenberg. *The Vanishing Adolescent*. Boston: Beacon Press, 1960.

23. Dennis Gabor. *Inventing the Future*. New York: Alfred A. Knopf, 1964.

24. James J. Gallagher. "Productive Thinking." *Review of Child Development Research: Volume I*. New York: Russell Sage Foundation, 1964. p. 349-81.

25. John W. Gardner. *Excellence: Can We Be Equal and Excellent Too?* New York: Harper & Brothers, 1961. p. 154.

26. *Ibid.*, p. 141.

27. John W. Gardner. *Self-Renewal, The Individual and the Innovative Society*. New York: Harper & Row, 1963.

28. John I. Goodlad. *School Curriculum Reform in the United States*. New York: The Fund for the Advancement of Education, March 1964.

29. J. P. Guilford, P. R. Merrifield and Anna B. Cox. "Creative Thinking in Children at the Junior High School Levels." U.S. Office of Education, Coopera-

tive Research Project No. 737. *Reports from the Psychological Laboratory*, No. 26. Los Angeles: The University of Southern California, September 1961.

30. Aldous Huxley. *Island*. New York: Harper & Row, 1962.

31. Julian Huxley. "Evolution and Genetics." *What Is Science?* James R. Newman, editor. New York: Harper & Brothers, 1955. p. 288.

32. Julian Huxley, editor. *The Humanist Frame*. New York: Harper & Brothers, 1961.

33. Julian Huxley. "The Humanist Frame." *The Humanist Frame*. Julian Huxley, editor. New York: Harper & Brothers, 1961.

34. *Innovation and Experiment in Education*. A Progress Report of the Panel on Educational Research and Development to the U.S. Commissioner of Education, the Director of the National Science Foundation, and the Special Assistant to the President for Science and Technology. Washington, D.C.: U.S. Government Printing Office, March 1964.

35. Donald W. MacKinnon. "The Nature and Nurture of Creative Talent." *American Psychologist* 17: 484-95; July 1962.

36. David Mallery. *High School Students Speak Out*. New York: Harper & Row, 1962.

37. Abraham Maslow. *Motivation and Personality*. New York: Harper & Brothers, 1954.

38. Abraham Maslow. Paper delivered at the American Personnel and Guidance Association Annual Meeting, April 12, 1965, Minneapolis, Minnesota.

39. Abraham Maslow. *Toward a Psychology of Being*. Princeton, New Jersey: An Insight Book, D. Van Nostrand Co., Inc., 1962.

40. *Ibid.*, p. iii.

41. *Ibid.*

42. Margaret Mead. *Continuities in Cultural Evolution*. New Haven: Yale University Press, 1964. p. xxi. Reprinted by permission of Yale University Press. Copyright 1964 by Yale University.

43. *Ibid.*, p. 239.

44. Lewis Mumford. *The Conduct of Life*. New York: Harcourt, Brace and World, Inc., 1951. p. 36.

45. Ralph H. Ojemann. "The Human Relations Program at the State University of Iowa." *Basic Approaches to Mental Health in the Schools*. A reprint series from the *Personnel and Guidance Journal*. Washington, D.C.: American Personnel and Guidance Association, 1960.

46. Donald Oliver. Harvard Graduate School of Education.

47. Robert Oppenheimer. "The Tree of Knowledge." *Harper's Magazine* 217: 55-60; October 1958.

48. Oliver L. Reiser. "The Integration of Knowledge." *The Humanist Frame*. Julian Huxley, editor. New York: Harper & Brothers, 1961. p. 233-50.

49. Anne Roe. Interview with Dr. Anne Roe, Professor, Harvard University, in conjunction with the preparation of a style-of-life film featuring her as a role model for the *Being and Becoming Film Series*.

50. Carl R. Rogers. *On Becoming a Person.* Boston: Houghton-Mifflin Co., 1961.

51. Nevitt Sanford. "Will Psychologists Study Human Problems?" *American Psychologist* 20: 192-203; March 1965. p. 201.

52. J. Richard Suchman. *The Elementary School Training Program in Scientific Inquiry,* Title VII, Project No. 216, N.D.E.A., Grant No. 7-11-038, June 1962. Urbana, Illinois: University of Illinois Press, 1963.

53. *Ibid.*

54. Hilda Taba, S. Levine and E. F. Freeman. *Thinking in Elementary School Children.* Cooperative Research Program Report No. 1574, U.S. Office of Education. San Francisco, California: San Francisco State College, 1963.

55. Robert Theobald. "Cybernation—Threat and Promise." *The Bulletin of the National Association of Secondary-School Principals* 48: 22-36; November 1964.

56. Robert Theobald. *Free Men and Free Markets.* New York: Clarkson M. Potter, Inc., 1963.

57. Paul Tillich. *The Courage To Be.* New Haven: Yale University Press, 1952.

58. E. Paul Torrance. *Guiding Creative Talent.* Englewood Cliffs, New Jersey: Prentice-Hall, Inc., 1962.

59. Arthur I. Waskow. "Young America's Newest Vocation." *Saturday Review* 48: 12-14, 52-53; June 5, 1965.

60. Robert W. White. *Lives in Progress.* New York: Holt, Rinehart and Winston, 1952. p. 3-4. Copyright 1952 by Robert W. White. Reprinted by permission of Holt, Rinehart and Winston, Inc.

61. *Ibid.,* p. 4.

Learning and Becoming—
New Meanings to Teachers

The learner is an active agent who organizes the world by labeling and grouping, noting and establishing relationships, and by hypothesizing and predicting. Thus the pupil creates his world and is not totally dependent upon his world to shape and mold him. Yet, in order to create the kind of environment conducive to learning and mental health, certain conditions are necessary.

Those conditions which give rise to productive learning are qualitatively and quantitatively rich experiences; human support and responsiveness to others, and opportunities for the learner to mediate these experiences through conversation. The school may, and perhaps even must, provide all three of these conditions in order to make possible change in one's cognitive field and in one's behavior.

6

Learning and Becoming—
New Meanings to Teachers

Marie M. Hughes

IT IS the hope of the authors of this volume that it may serve as a source book of present day thinking about growth and learning of significance to the teaching profession.

This chapter presents some meanings and implications for teaching gleaned from the foregoing chapters. The illustrations are designed to invite the reader to examine his present beliefs regarding learning and the processes by which an individual becomes what he presently is, and what he *may* become. Such an examination by a teacher of his beliefs may give him a firmer base on which to make professional decisions and may even clarify his concept of the ultimate purposes of the school experience. It is also conceivable that his own commitment as a teacher may be deepened as he understands more about the educative process; therefore, he can be more optimistic regarding the potential of human beings.

The Modifiability of Intelligence

The concept of an individual's becoming expressed as a process of interaction with his environment suggests different educational procedures from those compatible with the concept of the individual as "unfolding" in accordance with predetermined ability.

Data presented in Chapter 3 show this latter concept as no longer tenable. The kinds of activities and objects encountered, the kinds of human relationships and situations experienced make a difference in the competence and attitudes of an individual. These factors cannot be predetermined. From the time of birth the individual is trying to make sense out of his world. He is the active agent who organizes the world by categorizing and grouping, noting and establishing relationships, hypothesizing and predicting. He *makes his own world* through his processing, utilizing and retrieving information stored within his mind along with information he receives from outside and inside himself.

It may be interesting to look at young children to see how they function in encounters with their environments.

Recently it was possible to observe two little girls, one not yet three and the other just turned five, as they went about gaining and processing information from their environment. The specific environment was a large yard with two brick terraces and a fish pond with three indifferent goldfish. At first the girls were content to watch the fish, lifting the lily pads to see them more clearly. Next they followed the contours of the walks that took them from one side of the house to another. They climbed, walked and jumped off the wall of the treewell. Then the swing was tried out. Yes, two could sit in the basket swing. How about standing up in the basket? The curved surface thwarted them, and their attempt to stand was aborted. Next, experimentation with the tea cart which did nicely as a bus; moreover, it had two decks.

Time out for a little conversation with their father who was building the new flower bed. "Why did you do that?" "What goes in this hole?" "Here is a bug. Does he like the leaf? Where is his house?" The conversation was terminated when the girls' attention was attracted to a lizard darting about; they made a hopeless chase.

Later the girls found a bag of clothespins. For quite a period of time they occupied themselves pinning leaves on the back of the two plastic-laced chaise lounge. The rows of "clothes" were even and exact.

When the lawn sprinkler system was turned on, the five-year-old girl systematically tested her control of each of the four heads by placing her foot in various positions on top of the head. Her delight in the change in the flow of the water was a joy to watch.

Here in this encounter with a limited environment we saw two little girls using it in their own ways for their own purposes. Some aspects of the environment were new and some familiar. The basket swing afforded them some information about curved surfaces; their use of the tea cart was the familiar use of anything with wheels; however, the conventional purpose of such a piece of furniture was not disclosed to them. Their inventiveness with the clothespin play, using leaves for clothes, and the laced chair back for clothesline demonstrated something of the creativity inherent in all children. In this same episode the girls displayed a self-discipline in following the model of mother hanging up clothes. Thus the "clothes" placed in a straight line may be interpreted as more than mere pleasure in manipulative activity.

Two more features in this environmental encounter of the two little girls are worthy of mention: One, the involvement of the "whole child." In this case, the cliché is used advisedly. The children were responding as total organisms. They used muscles and mind; they experienced a gamut of feeling in direct relationship to what they were doing. Certainly they derived kinesthetic pleasure and satisfaction from many of their activities. They were mildly frustrated in their attempts to stand up on the curved surface of the basket swing and in their attempt to catch the lizard. They were gratified in their father's response to their questions and in their control over their environment—pushing the tea cart, swinging, and regulating the flow of water. In addition, they had choice of activity with freedom to explore as fancy dictated. Secondly, they made use of language to interact with one another and to *gain* more *information* from their environment. They had an adult who listened and responded to them. These children were moving toward their environment instead of away from it or against it (5).

It is from thousands of similar encounters that the child becomes what he is. What he thinks of himself, his openness to experience, his store of concepts, his way of organizing his world, his cognitive processes, his habits of reality testing, his recognition of his feelings, and his acceptance of his feelings are all an outgrowth of his transactions with his environment.

The differences in the life experiences of individuals begin early. The embryo and fetus are protected intrauterine, but the facts of impairment caused by rubella (German measles) and the drug, thalidomide, have told us that development does not unfold according to genetic plan *unless the environment is propitious.* There is an interactive factor even intrauterine.

The effects of the earliest days and weeks of life are indicated by Lawrence K. Frank in his discussion of the mother's handling of the infant during feeding:

This tactual stimulation is obtained from close contact with the mother's person, especially during breast feeding, when the infant receives both nutritional and tactual stimulation. It should be noted that the mother usually accompanies these tactual ministrations with soothing auditory stimuli, this provides the essentials for the child to use auditory stimuli in place of tactual stimuli as sources of adjustment. Thus, when the infant is weaned and more or less suddenly deprived of access to the mother's person (although her mothering may be otherwise continued), he is partially prepared to use the auditory stimuli of approval and reassuring words as substitutes for tactual stimuli. If he is successful in meeting this problem he will learn then to use auditory stimuli as sources of adjustment and to accept them for an ever-widening number and variety of persons. Concomitantly he will develop a susceptibility to auditory stimuli of a disapproving and threatening character. In this process we see the beginning of the individual's dependence upon the verbal reactions of others to his behavior, which plays so large a part in social relationships and the personality development of later years. Gestures and facial expressions of others are likewise implicated (3).

One can but ask, what of the children who habitually receive their bottle from a stuffed dog or some other inanimate object!

Effects of Environmental Encounters

The richness of some children's environment may be seen from this episode of a three year old boy who played with a canvas laundry bag attached to a stand-up frame. The bag accidentally fell over and the young boy immediately made it a boat. He climbed in and out of it. Finally he shifted his play, approaching and withdrawing from the opening of the bag that had now become the mouth of an alligator. His father and mother entered into the play, talking with him as though he were in the boat and, later, afraid of the alligator.

The significance of play accompanied by the approval of parent or other adult cannot be overestimated. The parent, by taking the role assigned to him by the child, demonstrates his interest and approval. For example, the parent may say to the boy with the boat, "Where are you going?" "How many people on your ship?" If the child is timid and the request to speak seems to cause anxiety, the parent may say, "My! You have a good boat." "You are a fine boatman." "You are making your boat go fast."

The significance of the parent's participation in play episodes then has two facets, one of approval and empathy with the child; second, that of use of language to mediate and extend the experience for the child. Teachers, particularly those with young children from disadvantaged homes, serve the same function. To make up for gaps in such situations, teachers give more time to play than is usual in a regular classroom.

Bower's statement of the importance of early years is this:

One of the prime purposes of the family is to provide the child with sufficient affective nutrient and home base support so that, as he grows, he feels safe enough to risk exploring the real and symbolic world around him. The health agencies provide basic biological, developmental and—where necessary—medical guidance to produce the physical and mental robustness required to take the normal risks of life. The play agencies (including informal play groups) provide the group experiences prerequisite to the use of symbols. With these three "givens," home, health and play experience, education can proceed at a merry and productive pace.[1]

There is a probability that as many as half the children entering school come from deprived environments of one kind or another. Earlier chapters have indicated something of the results of deprivation. The sources of deprivation are many.

Some children have had too many *do's*. "Do act like a lady." "Say how do you do to Mrs. L." "Do try to skate gracefully." "Do learn the names of the flowers in the garden." "Do practice your music lesson."

Some children have not been able to explore their environment because of the *don't's*. "Don't climb the tree." "Don't play in the water." "Don't talk to Mr. B., you will bother him."

Some children have lived in meager environments with too few objects, and slight variety in situations. For them many common aspects of the broader culture have never been encountered. Most of all, perhaps, the significant people in their lives are tired with feelings of discouragement and even hopelessness. The use of language has been minimal, often limited to directions and concrete questioning. Children from such families know little of play with words or conversation that has no excuse except the pleasure afforded by the exploration of ideas.

Some children have lived with warm, responsive adults who have talked with them and introduced them to an ever wider aspect of their environment. For such children, their encounters have included the sea and the mountain, the city and the country, animals and gardens, the airplane and the boat, the young and the old.

A young three year old from a rich environment of people who cared and who had provided many experiences for him proposed this question to his grandmother, "What do you do, grandma, when you run out of fingers to count?" This development of the concept of number as being more than ten fingers was interesting; equally interesting, however, was the *gap* in his understanding of the world disclosed a few weeks earlier. From babyhood he had been familiar with airplanes taking off and landing as well as their frequent passing overhead. He was present when his grandmother was seen off on a flight to another city. When the plane was

[1] Eli M. Bower. "The Achievement of Competency." Chapter 2. p. 24.

out of sight, he became very anxious and wanted to know how his grandmother "was going to get down." Even though he had witnessed planes taking off and landing since babyhood, the total process appeared not to be assimilated until his grandmother's return when he witnessed *her* coming down the steps.

The child's world and his attainment of the concepts that enable him to organize it are now still largely unknown. Because of this our educational programs are often less successful than we had hoped. It seems clear that two questions must be asked in regard to each child: What is the nature of his environmental encounters? and What concepts and attitudes is he in process of building through these encounters? Would the school program contribute more to the child's intellectual development if we were able to provide a match between the child's mental schemata and experience so that he could assimilate more? Or, on the other hand, would this intellectual growth be enhanced if we were able to provide the child with *experience* with dissonant data—something so different from what he has within his mental schemata that he must completely reorganize his schemata to accommodate the new data?

Hunt has already envisioned the possibilities in the new views on intelligence.*

It might be feasible to discover ways to govern the encounters that children have with their environments, especially during the early days of their development, to achieve a substantially higher intellectual capacity. Moreover, inasmuch as the optimum rate of intellectual development would mean also self-directing interest and curiosity and genuine pleasure in intellectual activity, promoting intellectual development properly need imply nothing like the grim urgency which has been associated with "pushing" children. Furthermore, these procedures, insofar as they tended to maximize each child's potential for intellectual development would not decrease individual differences in intellectual capacity as assessed by texts but would increase them (6).

The research task of discovering effective ways of governing children's environmental encounters, and of translating such knowledge into child rearing and other educational practices is stupendous. Nevertheless, it is not too early for teachers to begin some urgent modifications of their practices. The conclusion made by Deutsch may be strong enough, when related to data presented in earlier chapters of this yearbook, to spur us to additional effort:

Examination of the literature yields no explanation or justification for any child with an intact brain, and who is not severely disturbed, not to learn all the

---

* J. McV. Hunt. *Intelligence and Experience.* Copyright © 1961 The Ronald Press Company.

basic scholastic skills. The failure of such children to learn is the failure of the schools to develop curricula consistent with the environmental experiences of the children and their subsequent initial abilities and disabilities (2).

When the view is accepted that the child, at any point in time, is the product of his *unique* interactions with his unique environment, we have more understanding of differences and more hope for what the child may yet become. This understanding of the process of becoming provides clues to the kind of program-development in the school that may contribute most to the growth of a competent, self-fulfilled individual. At the very least, the view presented may help us avoid some errors of the past.

Once Again: Individual Differences

An error commonly made is that of labeling an individual as lazy, slow, not wanting to learn, stupid, immature, and so forth. Labels often seem to have the power to evoke from us as teachers the kind of behavior toward a child that is congruent with the labels we have attached to him. Most of us accept the fact that rats have less feeling and less intelligence than humans and yet a study shows that when one experimenter was told that he had a group of "smart" rats and another experimenter was told that he had a group of "stupid" rats, the rats subsequently learned maze running as "smart" and "stupid" rats (10). The inference being that the experimenters acted toward the rats and expected them to act in accordance with the labels given them.

Our grouping practices, our devotion to the infallibility of the first intelligence score that appears in the child's record folder, attest to our insensitivity to human potential. We know children are very different but we have not yet learned to live and work with the differences in comfortable and constructive ways.

Perhaps we have seen differences only in the ability to learn what we wanted the children to learn; moreover, our responses to children have tended to be judgmental. This evaluation is expressed in the way we sort out (group) children in a hierarchy. There are groups 1, 2, 3, 4, etc. In one high school, seven classification levels were maintained. What might happen, if, instead of judging children so arbitrarily, we were creative in providing *new* kinds of opportunities for them? In addition, suppose we were patient and supportive of children as they went about finding their *own ways* into the school situation?

It is difficult for us to comprehend the great differences even among young children entering school for the first time. For example, a study [2]

[2] Marie M. Hughes and Ruth Gates. "The Responses of Kindergartners to Selected Concepts." Unpublished Study. Salt Lake City: University of Utah, 1963.

of 70 kindergarten children of similar socioeconomic status divided equally as to sex showed, as expected, pronounced differences among the children. For example, in their responses to words they did not know. A few children said "My Mommy never told me." Others spoke matter-of-factly in a firm tone of voice with an "I don't know," and still others whispered, "I don't know," and some just looked without sound or movement.

Lois Murphy recently described in poetic fashion the ways young children meet new situations.

For one child to whom newness has progressively brought new satisfactions, a strange new experience arouses fantasies of new opportunities and potential fun; for another, strangeness brings potential ogres in its shadows. For still another, strangeness is simply a question mark, something to discover; this child will let strangeness have a fair chance. He allows it to show its colors; he does not prejudge it. One child may march forward, ready to beard a lion in his den if need be, while another skips into newness as if it carried a rainbow's promise of a pot of gold. Still another is transfixed and immobilized, seemingly hypnotized by inscrutable forces in strangeness itself (9).

It seems so obvious that children responding in such different ways cannot be treated alike or be subjected to the same expectations. It seems equally obvious that the range of situations offered within the classroom must be broad instead of limited and stereotyped as they most often are.

If one of our first errors in working with children is that of categorizing and labeling them, a second error is that of keeping all of them in the same kind of situation. We are eager for children to get into reading books, to move them into a next upward step in arithmetic, to write longer paragraphs, to read history instead of stories of horses. In other words, we want them to progress upward in an unbroken and fairly steep path. Such expectations are not in harmony with the ways of growth—growth is uneven, sometimes it even appears to show regression. A child who has been writing for some weeks may have a few days during which he asks the teacher to write for him. Children who have been choosing to read quite difficult books may change to reading old stories with simpler plots expressed in limited vocabularies.

Most classrooms make no allowance for such facts of development Children are evaluated as not doing well when they fluctuate in this manner. They are judged as contrary or uncooperative. In fact, all children who do not learn the material required in a grade by a specific teacher are considered not bright. Most career teachers are surprised when their "not bright" pupils do so well in their life work. If the school were more sensitive to individual differences, how many more people might come nearer self-fulfillment?

Kubie has pointed out the stultifying effects of our repetitive ways of doing things.

Limitless repetition without the guidance of insight is merely self-defeating; it does deeper damage by hampering spontaneous "intuitive," i.e., preconscious functions. There is considerable evidence that the freer is the learning process from neurotic distortion, and the less obstructed it is by counter-processes which are rooted in unconscious conflicts (i.e., the more "normal" it is), the less repetition is needed. Nevertheless in the acquisition of any skill, whether manipulative, symbolic, or instinctive, the teacher continues to place major emphasis on repetitive drill (7).

The above quotation implies that we give more of the same kind of material when the child does not seem to be getting it. In no school situation has this procedure been more persistent than in beginning reading instruction. We continue to present the same words in the same kind of drill lesson. When children are not responding positively, should we not change the situation for them? Only in this way do they have an opportunity for new perceptions.

If children are to be involved in their own learning so that learning moves forward with attention, zest and satisfaction, the use of situations requiring repetitive, automatic responses must be curtailed. Most drill requires such responses. As Kubie argues, traditional drill may not be warranted to the degree its prevalence in the schools indicates. The readers of this report can be heard saying, "But we need drill. Some things have to be automatic." Once again we reiterate that the issue is one of deliberate, discriminative judgment on the part of the teacher. The records of classrooms show that drills on small numbers with a ritualistic statement of the problem, on naming the colors, on parts of words, and so forth, are insistent.

Such lessons involve a group of children who must listen to the same thing over and over again. Many children have mastered such content before they entered school. It is true that they might take comfort and gain confidence by doing something they can do but at what point do they become bored? Who becomes bored first? Which ones need a challenge? How does the teacher know? What practice will children do on their own? What opportunities are there for needed individual practice? Such questions as these call for decision making of the highest professional caliber. No preconceived notion of a nicely ordered sequence and ritual of presentation of content will provide the basis for the proper decision.

For example, as we have watched children learn to read, the limitations of the usual beginning reading activities used in a routine manner have become apparent. There are genuine differences in attitudes toward books among those children who have had large numbers of books and stories and those whose contacts with books have been meager. Moreover, some children have the rewards of reading opened to them through the use of *other* materials. For one child it was the record of the antics of the loved golden hamster; for another it was captioned photographs of activities of himself and classmates; for still another it was a cookbook.

Children have to find some personal satisfaction in reading before they give sufficient attention to it to really learn to read.

With older children or youth, the availability of a historical novel or a journal of an explorer has been known to change attitudes toward history.

When teachers are asked to identify the situations in which there is the greatest pupil involvement, the response is always when they are talking about themselves, what they have done and what they have, what they want and what they are going to do. Obviously an educational program cannot be carved exclusively from this kind of discussion. What is the bridge to the wider world and what are the processes that may guide creative classroom teaching?

Processes and Principles Which Promote Productive Learning Situations

The space provided by one chapter does not permit a complete exposition of useful processes and principles, if such were possible to give. Nevertheless, the author has selected a few processes and principles [3] to discuss. These are: (a) models of human activity and feeling; (b) pacing; (c) choice; (d) challenge; and, (e) teacher responsiveness to the individual.

Models of Human Activity and Feeling

Any thinking about or discussion of models tends to slide over into the deeper and highly significant psychological process of personal identification. There are, of course, various degrees of identification. Models in this discussion are used more in the sense of becoming aware of something to the extent that one imitates it. The imitation is limited to a skill or a particular way of doing things, although the model may become,

---

[3] The distinction between processes and principles as applied to teaching is not explicated. The complexity of teaching in its simultaneity of events and interrelations makes talking about it without oversimplification difficult at this point in our conceptualizations and theorizing. I do not wish to simplify what is even more complex than I wish to acknowledge.

for a few children, a person for identification. If we consider models in a wider context we might say that the individual's "awareness" of something additional or different makes possible a change in his cognitive field, which in turn, as Snygg suggests, results in a change in his behavior.

Disadvantaged children, for example, have had little or no contact with puzzles, word games, "book" games of the old "authors" type, or those built on the old "parcheesi" formula.

These games may be made available in the classroom, but there are no "takers" until the children see the games in use. In our own experience, teaching the games to somewhat older children who then use the materials unobstrusively in the classroom, generates in the younger children an interest in learning the games. Under this condition they will give the necessary attention to learning the games themselves. The presence of the model using the materials results in awareness and interest in doing it oneself. The new skill in turn becomes self-satisfying and provides another building block in a feeling of adequacy and control—a step toward more mature competence.

Of course, models of activities go beyond games. We have noticed in Operation Head Start classes that the young Spanish-speaking boys tended to avoid certain activities. Few boys joined the playhouse play, or made collages using colored tissue paper, or worked with the weaving of mats. However, this was not true in the classes where the male student aide had participated in these activities. It was also noted that after the activity was thus legitimatized, the boys chose it on their own.

This past year a ninth grade class of limited achievement spent three hours a day in a special program at the University Experimental Learning Center. One of the fruitful experiences for them proved to be their access to the Education Instructional Library. Here they found an unusually fine collection of books, but more particularly, they found college students studying. It was amusing to watch individuals assume the sitting posture of a bearded but serious student reading or writing. Incidentally, most of the 45 ninth graders became quite skilled in the use of the card catalogue. Their personal practice certainly began by imitation. They had been markedly inattentive during an initial instruction period but when they *asked for help,* they gave attention.

The presence of models of activity provides an *invitation*. When help is available to give the necessary demonstration and aid to children to enable them to participate, some salient elements of a productive learning situation are present. The potency of the presence of models suggests that a wider age range as well as a wider range of permissible activities might be one way to move toward a more productive learning situation.

Pacing

Another element necessary in the productive learning situation is that of pacing. My own conviction is that each learner will proceed further if he does his own pacing in moving into more difficult work and moving into new situations. No other person can know the fears and constrictions of another. This principle of instructional pacing is based upon the assumption that the possibilities for more difficult work, more responsibility, and so forth are always present.

The concept of pacing is often confused with a *laissez faire* permissiveness. This is not what is meant. The teacher holds an expectation of growth and more complex behavior for the child. He has a belief in the capacity of the child and the conviction that he will perform in a different manner when it is possible for him to do so. These convictions are conveyed to the child, yet at the same time his autonomy is respected. The issuing of the invitation to more difficult work (new situations), the proffering of aid, the support offered, and the acceptance of the child as he is with what he finds it possible to do, require a quality of sensitivity, skill and judgment that is needed in few other human situations. This is teaching.

Choice

The relationship of choice or self-pacing is readily apparent; however choice involves an awareness of several alternatives. As an ultimate it pertains to what one dreams and plans to make of himself. On an everyday functioning basis in the classroom it means choosing to practice with arithmetic drill sheets or the teaching machine, or working out the report on the cost of fencing and landscaping the schoolyard.

Choice in the classroom may involve the editing of the play for an assembly. "What scenes tell the story? What needs to be eliminated or expanded? Who will have what part?" Choice may be strictly personal, "Shall I write to Aunt Kate or finish reading my book?" Choice must be made with consideration for one's responsibility to others; also, it must be made in reference to time available to one, to skills one has or wants, and to one's goals. The school provides alternatives in activities, helps to clarify values and goals and the means of reaching such goals. Choice may be given on the level of an open assignment—we need more . . . ; it may be given in terms of the order in which one may do that which is structured and required; it may be given in situations of slight valence to one, or it may be a situation of major significance, but the *ultimate* choice of each individual relates to what he chooses to become. Herbert Bonner holds a view of man as "seeker after values which he sets for himself. From this point of view, more important than tranquility, security, and survival is the individual's desire to fulfill himself as a unique person" (1). Each child needs to know himself and have respect for what he is and what he may become. The school program can contribute to an individual's feelings of confidence, to his skills of study, and to his basic attitudes toward himself and the world. It can help him clarify his values and goals. It can help him sense what it is to be a human being with the capacity for a range of feeling responses and mental operations.

Challenge

Much emphasis has been placed on choice and self-pacing. It should be noted, however, that these processes cannot be very meaningful to the children when the choice given by the teacher is only on the level of "What song do you wish to sing?" The classroom offerings should not be repeated day after day. The program should offer new opportunities and new vision to the student. What is a challenge to one naturally will not be to another. Challenge as used here is not a dare or a bet. It is an expansion; it is awareness at a greater depth. To challenge a student is to give him a new weapon or instrument that increases his own power. This may be a computation skill or a series of facts from which he can derive new relationships. One of our records of a third grade discussion reveals an opportunity that was ignored by the teacher.

Third grade—23 students—30 minutes

TEACHER: How many of you enjoyed our trip yesterday out to Escalante Valley? That's fine. What did you learn new that you had never seen before?

MICHAEL: I seen a lot of potatoes.

TEACHER: Speak right up.

MICHAEL: I saw how they packed them and how they put them in the truck and washed them.

TEACHER: Speak right up.

DAVID: I saw how they put them in the big gunny sacks.

CATHY: I saw how they washed them.

KAREN: I saw how they hurried and picked them up.

TEACHER: Did you think the lady that was right close to us was working really hard when she picked up potatoes?

CHILDREN: Yes.

TEACHER: *What makes you think she was really working hard? Bobby?*
BOBBY: *Because she sort of had sweat on her forehead.*
NEIL: I saw how they dumped potatoes.
TEACHER: Where?
NEIL: I saw how they dumped them.
TEACHER: Dumped them where? Where did you see them dump potatoes?
NEIL: In a truck.
TEACHER: In a truck.
DAVID: The lady who picks them up, she bends over and her back gets sore.
TEACHER: I imagine it would.
LARRY R: I seen 'em. I seen.
TEACHER: I saw.
LARRY R: I saw where this tractor picked them up and dumped them on the ground again.
TEACHER: The tractor dug them and dumped them on the ground. Bobby?
BOBBY: I thought it was neat the way they went and hooked the machine on the truck and the man went and dumped in the potatoes into the thing that went into the bin.
MICHAEL: *We could tell she was tired at how fast she was picking up and she was always breathing a big deep breath.*
TEACHER: *A big deep breath. And what would she do when she would get the sack full?*
MICHAEL: She would set it down and then she would go and take the sack off her back and hook it on the front and start picking them up again.
TEACHER: It looked like a big skirt, didn't it?
CHILD: She sure filled it fast.
TEACHER: Very fast.

The italicized statements have significance for our discussion. Here are concrete observations of children from which they inferred that the woman who picked up potatoes worked hard. Might it not have challenged the children to learn something of their mental processes and to acquire the new word *infer?* The simple recital of what they had seen could have been given by an alert five or six year old; these children were eight.

Children's ideas are often challenged by the ways some members of the group play unfinished stories. Under this situation new ways of acting are introduced and different values are disclosed.

Children can be challenged by learning the differences between *facts*, as they are generally agreed upon by scholars in the field or objective observers, and *opinions* expressed by themselves and others either orally or in the printed word. Few classrooms bring this kind of challenge to children. Moreover, records of classroom discourse show that teachers seldom make such distinctions in their own work. For example, a question of fact is asked and a reply of opinion is accepted. Comparisons and judgments are rendered without making overt the criteria used. Would not children be challenged to find what different judgments result when the criteria are changed?

Another source of challenge in the classroom is the child who thinks in an original manner. Such a child's remarks are very often declared "out of field."

It appears from our reading of hundreds of records of classroom discourse that the teachers who are unaccepting of the challenge presented by a new line of thought are immersed in their own "set" or plan of what ought to be. In other words, they are not alert to the numerous possibilities open in the situation. One of our sixth grade records demonstrated this. The discussion pertained to the opening to the public of Lake Powell at Glen Canyon Dam. The teacher asked the question, "What will this big lake mean to us?" Several students responded with some aspects of the new recreational opportunities, but one youngster began to talk about business possibilities. "Someone could buy up the land and build cabins." Another student talked of buying boats to rent and someone mentioned a snack bar. This part of the discussion was "nipped" by the teacher, who said, "We are not going to talk about business but how we can have recreation on Lake Powell." The limiting we do thoughtlessly, often prevents what might be new thinking or a challenge to members of the group.

Responsiveness to Others

No discussion of present concepts of teaching and learning can be completed without giving attention to communication in the classroom. There is need of an opportunity for dialogue and there is need to raise the quality of dialogue. Speech has both an outer meaning that is purely descriptive and an inner (personal) meaning. To respond constructively to children (and others) requires that one actively listens for the meaning of the other. Such concentrated listening indicates a caring for the other. A few simple examples: the young child brought a furry caterpillar crawling up his arm for his mother to see: "Look," he said, "it is striped, it is beautiful." And the mother replied, "Go wash your dirty hand." Another child high on the ladder called to his mother and said, "Look at me. I'm at the very top. I did it all by myself." But the mother said, "Get down this minute before you fall."

Tom, a new boy in school, was asked along with the rest of the sixth grade to write a composition. Everyone got busy but Tom who just sat. After a time, the teacher became aware of this and came over to suggest that he get busy or he would be left behind. He replied, "We didn't do much writing at that other school." Teacher continued, "You could write about Thursday's ball game or our party, yes, write about our party with Mrs. Johnson's room." The teacher went on her way and Tom still sat.

Tom's statement, "We didn't do much writing at the other school." was a factual, reality statement, but what was he saying, what was the personal meaning? "I'm homesick for my old school." "I'm scared." Maybe he was even saying, "I really don't know a thing about writing." or perhaps, "I don't think I'll ever be as good as these kids seem to be."

Always we work in a context of *personal meaning* schemata and a *cognitive-culture-oriented-meaning* schemata. It is necessary for us to listen to each person fully so we may experience the essence of the learner's expression.

Another teacher demonstrated her listening in an ordinary but important manner. Hazil was telling a long story about the pets at her home. Asked the teacher, "How many birds do you have at your house?"

HAZIL: We did have two, but Bedgie flew out and got lost.

TEACHER: Ah, not the one that went up your fingers.

HAZIL: Yes.

TEACHER: Oh, I hope you find it. Let us know, won't you?

Not only did the teacher hear the child this time, but she had heard the child previously. She conveyed her caring. Meerloo boldly writes, "Words are bodily contact. All speaking is opposing, fighting, loving" (8).

Listening must have a constancy about it, in order to have an authentic ring. It is really grounded in faith as to what the other may become. Teachers need such faith. They need to believe in a potential unrealized.

The two things a teacher (listener) most commonly does to foreshorten communication are: (a) rendering adverse judgment on what the person is saying before he understands what is said or meant; and (b) refusing to hear the speaker out before listening to our own thoughts and ideas. We immediately want to speak and tell *our own tale;* or we know the opposite of what the person is saying, so we wish to tell him about it. Either way, we begin listening to ourselves and forming our rebuttal so we never *hear* what was said. The lesson plan for the day is often slavishly followed and prevents the kind of dialogue that could extend and deepen meanings for all.

Jules Henry (4) has called attention to a third aspect in the classroom situation that prevents understanding. This is "noise" or the aspect of the message that is not intended. A short illustration demonstrates the point:

> Alice, who was trying to read, had difficulty with a word. Fred spoke up and told it to her. Whereupon, the teacher asked, "Fred, are you cooperating?" To this question he immediately replied, "No." The teacher went on to explain, "She won't know, and I won't know if she knows, and she won't know if she can learn if you tell her." The teacher then went ahead to give cues to Alice, but in the end the teacher had to tell her the words.

What did Fred learn? He can't help, but the teacher can. What did Alice learn? She is even dumber than she thought. What did both learn about the complex process of cooperation? Follow the rules of the teacher! How much "noise" of this kind is present in each classroom at all levels of instruction?

The importance of language to mental health and individual competence cannot be stressed too strongly. Language and touch are ways of relating to one another. When we are not heard—when no one listens, we feel unworthy, in error, afraid, unsure, and in the end our loneliness is increased.

The teacher who has listened and responded within the personal meaning of the child has made it more possible for the child to continue his learning and has left the child readier to accept and to cooperate with what the teacher has to offer tomorrow.

References

1. Herbert Bonner. *On Being Mindful of Man.* Boston: Houghton-Mifflin Company, 1965. p. 145.
2. Martin Deutsch. "Facilitating Development in the Pre-School Child: Social and Psychological Perspectives." *Merrill-Palmer Quarterly of Behavior and Development* 10(3) : 249-64; 1964. p. 258.
3. Lawrence K. Frank. "Management of Tension." *Society as the Patient.* New Brunswick, New Jersey: Rutgers University Press, 1948. p. 121-22.
4. Jules Henry. "The American Classroom." Chapter 8. *Culture Against Man.* New York: Random House, 1963.
5. Karen Horney. *Neurosis and Human Growth.* New York: W. W. Norton and Company, 1950.
6. J. McV. Hunt. *Intelligence and Experience.* New York: The Ronald Press Company, 1961. p. 363.

7. Lawrence Kubie. *Neurotic Distortion of the Creative Process*. Lawrence, Kansas: University of Kansas Press, 1958. p. 122-23. Quoted by permission of the University of Kansas Press.

8. Joost A. M. Meerloo. *Conversation and Communication: A Psychological Inquiry*. New York: International Universities Press, Inc., 1958. p. 18.

9. Lois Murphy *et al*. *The Widening World of Childhood*. New York: Basic Books, Inc., 1962. p. 193. Copyright © 1962 by Basic Books, Inc., Publishers.

10. Robert Rosenthal and Kermit Fode. "Experimenter Bias." *Behavioral Science* 8(3): 183-189; 1963.

The School and the Ego
As Information Processors

In order to live effectively, all organisms, whether they be basically social or biological in nature, must have adequate information. While it has often been said that bread is the staff of life, it is more accurate to say that information is the staff of life.

There is an analogy created between the processes by which the ego mediates or "screens" information (differentiation, fidelity testing, pacing, expansion, and integration) and the means by which an institution, such as a school, processes information. These "means" are properties indigenous to the discipline relatively new to education, "systems analysis." Some of these properties are independence, progressive segregation, adaptiveness, and stability.

The purpose in creating the analogy is to highlight the importance of the flow and control of information in a school. An equally important purpose is to offer to educators a new way of viewing and appraising those functions that are carried on in the school by administrators, teachers, pupils, and the various people who perform the support services.

7

The School and the Ego as Information Processors

Walter B. Waetjen and Kenneth C. Weisbrod

PREVIOUSLY, ego processes were described as serving as a mediation or screening agent operating between the individual's conceptual world of meaning and the world of available information. In this chapter, we will examine the ego intervention function as analogous to the role of that part of society called school in light of some "systems" properties.

We approach this task aware of the risk in taking some liberties with concrete technological concepts developed and employed by thoroughgoing systems analysts. We also recognize that in using systems concepts to examine human processes and systems language to describe them, some liberties may be taken with positions held by traditional educators. With apologies to both groups let us make clear at this point that a *system,* as the term will be used, simply refers to a set of operations which receive input and produce an output product. By focusing upon the system functioning as a whole, we plan to characterize the interacting subsystems as they effect change in the total system action.

The basic premise from which this discussion proceeds is that both the cognitive structure of an individual and the curriculum of a given school are respectively in effect an assemblage of interrelated entities or subsystems which function together as an organized whole to yield a product (behavior) which is unique to that assemblage.

This means that the cognitive structure of any given person is not necessarily a unitary thing but is made up of different parts; however, all the parts function together and, in the competent person, an effective behavior is the result. We may say the same thing about a school, for it, too, is an assemblage of different subsystems all of which are intended to produce some change in the behavior of pupils. That change in behavior we refer to as learning. Two of the subsystems in a school are the pupils and the teacher, who together make up the classroom unit within the school where the exchange of information between the teacher and pupils is of essential importance. Another subsystem is the faculty group, for this assemblage of persons develops many different kinds of information which are variously referred to as subject matter content, regulations, standard operating procedures, and the more unofficial, faculty lounge kinds of information (gossip, hearsay, and folklore) which nevertheless enter into the functioning of the school. We may identify other subsystems of the school by referring to administrative functions which are carried on in all schools. In our terms the administrative function is normally carried out by one person, the principal. The principal functions to generate information which is transmitted to the various other subsystems or parts of the total system which we are referring to as school.

A final subsystem of the school consists of a number of people providing supporting functions to the instructional and operational processes of the school. The environment in which the school functions is the community, representing the larger system, society. The community is in the constant process of exchanging information with the school in a variety of ways, that is, with pupils, with the teachers, and with school principals. It should be pointed out that the general objectives of all of the subsystems within the school or the "mission" of education, in systems language, are essentially the same as long as information is exchanged. The "mission" of education which we have in mind is the more effective functioning of the school so as to bring about more effective learning and more competent individuals.

It must be made clear that these different subsystems of the school may not necessarily be in agreement as to what better learning is or what the competent individual is. The competent functioning of the individual is dependent upon the orderly interaction of these component subsystems. Such interaction is made possible by the flow and control of information within, between and among individuals and groups of individuals comprising the total system. In other words, agreement depends upon the effective communication of information within and between the school and its environment.

The situation of man with respect to information is that he lives in two worlds, one public and one private.[1] The public world is the objective, material, outer world which exists around us regardless of what we know, feel or think about it. The private world is precisely what we do know, feel and think about the public world. The private world is the world as it seems to us. It is the conceptual world of meaning in which we most truly live. It is impossible for the inner world to embrace the whole of the outer world. It is important, however, that the inner world and the outer world correspond at least to some extent, because the individual's intellectual competence, his mental health and, indeed, his continued existence depend upon the validity of his private meaning relative to the objective events existing and occurring in the public world.

Lacking contact with adequate information concerning some aspects of the environment, the individual may acquire concepts which have little relevance to objective reality and which may even be false. With reference to our analogy, these ideas apply equally as well to a school as they do to the individual person's ego. It is important that the inner world and outer world of the school correspond to a fairly high degree. So, too, it is important that the school maintain contact and obtain adequate information from its environment in order to derive programs and operating procedures that are valid.

Information and Uncertainty

The concept of information is basic to systems thinking. It is the vehicle by which meaning is acquired and transmitted from one system to another. In its broadest sense, information may be thought of as energy, since some form of physical and/or psychological action is implied when information is communicated to a system capable of being affected by it. The criteria of capability of a given information system are: its existing capacity to exchange information with other systems in its environment; and its repertoire of stored information available for retrieval and production of competent, i.e., time and situation appropriate, behavior.

Our practical use of the term *information* denotes meaningful information which has significance for the receiver. Such information is sought for by the receiver. It is purposive and is goal-related, as opposed to being passively absorbed. Information for an individual exists on a one-to-one relationship with uncertainty. To be more exact, the kinds

[1] George Gaylord Simpson. *This View of Life.* New York: Harcourt, Brace & World, 1964.

and amounts of information received by an individual will be determined by the degree to which his uncertainty has been reduced. To put it still another way, the learner must experience some degree of anxiety or cognitive dissonance about something before he can learn anything about it. Information is something an individual looks for, listens for, or seeks through directly experiencing and questioning the world around him. From this point of view, school as an information processing system is successful in the extent that teachers are alert to the learners' current state of information deprivation or satiation concerning any given activity.

A host of other interesting implications for teaching and learning are introduced with the use of the term *information* when we consider the individual and the school as information processing systems. Before we deal with these, however, it may be desirable to clarify some aspects of *systems thinking*. First of all, the kind of system with which we are concerned is an open system. One premise of this discussion is that an open system tends to exchange information with other systems. This is readily observable and applicable to a given school when we note that the community members, the principal, the support services personnel and teachers of that school exchange information with their counterparts in other schools within the community. Also, there is an exchange of information with scholars, such as psychologists, sociologists, and subject matter specialists. These individuals provide meaningful information to the school concerning the learning, growth and development of students.

This exchange of information means that there is input and output in process continuously. In this respect a school can be described as "an open system," for it gives information as well as receives information. This giving and receiving helps the school to maintain itself in a relatively steady state. The term "steady state" could mislead one to believe that the school is static and unchanging. Actually, the term means that the school is in a steady state because it is constantly giving as well as receiving information. The school which is operating within a steady state is keeping abreast of changes and surges from its environment. In this respect the school may be seen as viable and adaptive, for it is producing an output which is consistent with the information it has been receiving. In the process of doing so, the school is modified by the environment in which it functions. School also modifies the environment, which in turn becomes more amenable to the school and therefore better accommodates the school as an interdependent system within the larger system: the community.

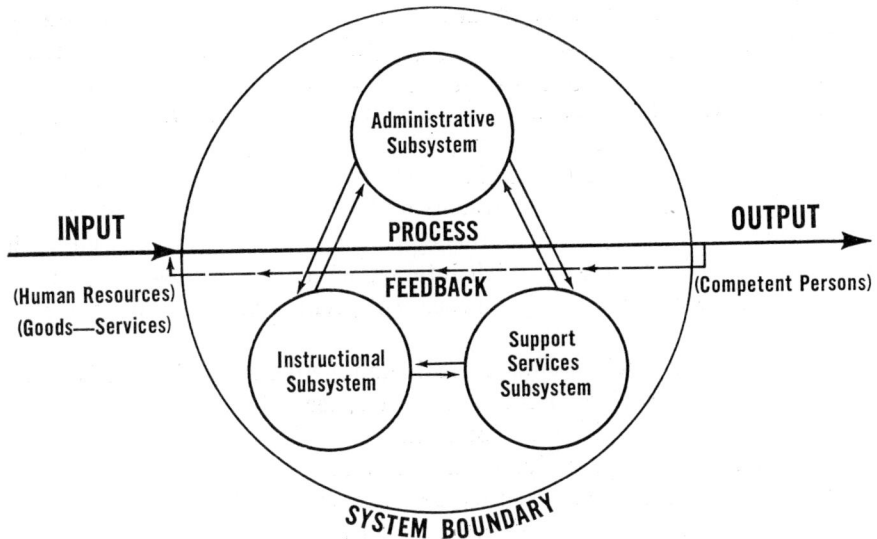

Diagram 1. A Typical Open System in Its Environment.

Attention is called to Diagram 1, which represents a typical open system in its environment. There are several characteristics worth noting. The system (school) has three major subsystems representing administration, instruction, and support services which interact as indicated by the arrows showing channels of information flow. The flow is essentially reciprocal since meaningful information flow is always a two-way process. Another major characteristic is indicated by the horizontal solid line running from the environment to output into the environment. The dotted line shows feedback which becomes input to the system's action. The implication here is that such a system is a self-adjusting, self-correcting system, that is, it modifies future processing of input material to produce an output product more consistent with environmental needs. Another characteristic shown is the system's boundary which differentiates system from environment, and the area labeled "process" comprising everything inside the system's boundaries. The boundaries of a system are seen as permeable to input and output information while process includes all intracommunication of information among and between subsystems.

The administration subsystem of a school is normally carried on by a principal and, perhaps, by a vice principal who initiate and coordinate action at a school policy planning, operations, and fiscal management level. They usually serve as well in supervisory and evaluative roles with respect to instruction and support services and interpret the system functions to the environment. Instruction subsystems comprise all of the teachers, each of whom represents a classroom which is another level of subsystems. The teacher in the classroom is a subsystem and each pupil is a subsystem, all of which interact with varying degrees of freedom within the classroom in the process of giving and receiving information.

The support services subsystem includes all nonadministrative and nonteaching personnel who interact with other subsystems to facilitate the flow and control of information in the process of improving the output product, i.e., competent individuals. A few of the school personnel comprising the support services subsystem are the curriculum consultants, counselors, child welfare personnel as well as people providing clerical, custodial, transportation, and food services.

At the risk of belaboring the obvious or becoming redundant, the overall purpose of this part of the discourse is to demonstrate the interaction of interdependent subsystems in the process of information exchange in order to produce a product.

When open systems are limited in their interaction, i.e., limited in the exchange of information, they tend toward rigidity. This is simply to say that when a school both gives and receives less information, it becomes less and less viable, with less and less capability of interaction. Viewed in this way, there is no alternative for the effective functioning of school but to exchange information among its subsystems as well as between the school and other agencies or systems outside the school.

Closed systems, including all machines, lack the capacity for interaction and the exchange of information and therefore are subject to the effects of the gradual dissipation of stored information (energy) until a state of equilibrium is reached. An important point pertinent to this discussion is that even open systems contain sources of rigidity and breakdown as well as capacities for adaptation and growth. This applies equally to the individual who maintains a closed mind and fails to recognize the implications for growth in the information available to him, as it does to the school which fails to recognize its need for modification of its functions to accommodate the output requirements and expectations of its environment.

The Systems Approach

Systems analysis is a way of looking at processes in relation to their purpose; hence, the purpose of systems analysis is an evaluative one. Outputs can be evaluated against these criteria: quality, quantity, and time. In other words, the system is expected to produce a certain output of a certain quality in a given period of time. For example, a school is expected to produce competent individuals with a certain amount of learning in a stipulated time.

Our present purpose is to examine the ego mediation processes, differentiation, fidelity, pacing, expansion, and integration, described in Chapter 2, by using the "systems approach," and applying these same mediation processes to the role of the school in society. As we have indicated, the process of interaction between and among systems and the resultant modification of the total system action reveal the direction and nature of impending change in the output of a given system.

The following structural properties may be seen as facilitating or inhibiting the effectiveness of ego mediation or education function moving from differentiation to increasing integration of information. These systems characteristics are equally applicable to a single subsystem or concept which in the total framework of concepts make up the self-system of an individual as they are to groups of individuals within the framework of the larger system representing a school. Before undertaking a detailed analysis of these mediation functions as they relate to systems action, it may be interesting to consider in a general way some fairly universal systems properties. These will serve to clarify ways in which a change in the relationship among the entities or subsystems influences the total systems action. The following are descriptions of eight such properties:

1. A system has *independence* to the extent that a change in one entity or subsystem effects change in that entity alone and does not effect change in the systems action. A totally independent system is a closed system and is destined to a state of equilibrium or complete loss of stored energy since there is no communication between its entities. In general, it can be stated that complete independence cannot exist among the biological systems, that is, open systems as long as life continues.

With respect to cognitive systems or their counterpart in society, the school, a possible exception might be the example of the serious psychopathological state, such as, schizophrenic reaction (catatonic type), in which independence is approached when the individual reaches the level of behavior where only the lower organic activities are maintained.

Another example would be a school classroom in which productive learning of the individual pupils has been thwarted by rigidly imposed rules and the threat of certain punishment.

2. A system is in a state of progressive *segregation* if in time the system tends toward independence. As communication between entities diminishes, the systems action tends to be more constricted. In other words, when communication is usually admitted to the cognitive structure and remains segregated from concepts already held, it is denied symbolic linkage and remains isolated or encapsulated, having little or no effect upon the systems action.

This would epitomize the behavior of a teacher who, having taken a number of child psychology courses, continues to evaluate pupil progress against a single standard. Thus, behavior may become progressively inconsistent with what the individual is presumed to have learned as the independent functioning of subsystems increases.

3. An *adaptive* system is one that changes in response to environmental change. In general, adaptiveness contributes to growth and productivity. On the other hand, some systems existing in a highly fluid environment may lack stability owing to limited internal integration. Conceivably an individual lacking the mediation functions of a strong ego might develop an overadaptive conceptual system. He might act impulsively to whims and be strongly influenced by the divergent opinions of others.

This is characteristically true of young children who have not yet reduced ambiguous information taken in at face value and who respond to its implication with behavior that is frequently inconsistent with its meaning. The function of fidelity testing would enable such individuals to effect environmental changes as well as to be affected by changes in the environment and therefore to behave with greater consistency in terms of information received. Another example might be a school principal who listens to a lay pressure group and immediately installs a new reading program without taking into account the effect which it will have upon other aspects of the curriculum.

4. A *stable* system is one which keeps its internal functions in a steady state. The stable system is free to give up or to modify entities as new ones are added. Highly integrative individuals operating under a minimum of threat can expand their competencies by acquiring new information even though it may be necessary to change some of their valued beliefs or biases in order to accommodate it.

A couple of examples might be the subject matter specialist who keeps current in a rapidly expanding field of knowledge, or a school which gains faculty and community support to modify its academic grading procedures in light of new and conclusive research findings. This implies a state of openness to change which requires the breaking down of new information into manageable amounts and admitting it to reality. It suggests as well the capacity to discharge stress induced by having to modify some previously held facts to accommodate new information which may be contrary to old information.

5. A system has *hierarchial order* if it continues a gradation of entities and relationships between entities. Under hierarchial order a system is in the process of expansion from lower to higher levels of integration. Change, in this instance, implies increasing communication from newly admitted information of a peripheral or tentative nature to higher levels more central to the cognitive field. The direction of change is toward wholeness which is the opposite of conditions under progressive segregation. The important ingredient here is a state of interdependence among subsystems or entities requiring a continuous flow of information to all entities and permitting the inclusion of new concepts and generalizations into the hierarchy of valued concepts.

6. A system is *degenerate* if it has independence in all relationships to all of its entities. The free flow and control of information is of central importance to systems action. Without this the input and output would be identical as though a pipeline were to flow through the system from the input to output. Hence, the processing of input (information) rests heavily upon the interaction of concepts or subsystems having gained at least some degree of integration. Although highly unlikely, the situation might be similar to that of an individual whose entire store of knowledge was gained by rote memorization, which he could recall and repeat verbatim. Such simply differentiated information might be received into the cognitive field or total system without meaning and be capable of producing little or no change in the behavior of the system.

7. A system has *progressive systemization* if in time independence tends toward wholeness. Such systems become progressively open to accommodate change in both the internal and external environments. The direction of change is toward higher levels of abstraction and interrelatedness together with increasing capacities to receive, incorporate and implement information taken into the system. The resultant output (behavior) would be more and more consistent with environmental demands for competence. Feedback to the system would become progressively supportive and reassuring of the systems action.

8. A system has *wholeness* if a change in any of the entities effects a change in all of the entities and a change in the systems action. Wholeness implies a maximum of effectiveness at the other end of the scale from independence and a functioning of a system completely competent to cope with all environmental demands. This is, of course, the seldom achieved goal of open systems. The important implication here is that all mediation processes would function with an unusually high degree of consistency and accuracy allowing for an almost complete matching between the worlds of inner meaning and of objective reality.

The School as a Processor and Generator of Information

Educators have long suspected that teaching involves more than telling. They have also become aware that perceiving is more than seeing and that learning involves more than just listening. It is unfortunate that these things are true, for if they were not true the task of the teacher would be exceedingly simple. He would need only to know his subject matter and to expound it at length in front of students who would then absorb each and every fact, concept, generalization and abstraction. The delightful consequence would be that we would have no underachievers and no learning disabilities. But the ego mediation processes, described in Chapter 2, clearly indicate that we cannot be this euphoric. Whatever information the individual learner receives from the external world is processed by him in rather selective ways. We can only find comfort in the fact that an individual thrives on information and he accepts information in selective ways.

In the sections that follow, we will examine ways in which the ego processes, described in Chapter 2, have counterparts which are properties indigenous to systems analysis. The purpose of these descriptions is not to suggest that a school has an ego, for we feel uncomfortable with such an attribution. On the other hand, since both the school and the ego create information as well as receive it, then to this extent the school functions in the community as the ego functions within the individual. By examining some of the processes and properties used for handling information by these two very different types of organisms, we can hopefully gain some new insights into the ways in which they operate.

Differentiation and Independence

When an individual is entering an entirely new field of learning, he may commonly encounter what is perceived to be a large, difficult and undifferentiated mass of information. This may be often only temporarily defeating to the learner, for he has already developed some strategies for grasping the "handles" of the new material. It is usually not long before he begins to isolate some events, processes and objects from the ambiguous mass to which he can attach meaning. While it can be said that the first step in learning is that of separating attractive items or bits of information from the generalized mass, such information serves no useful purpose in the modification of the learner's behavior, since information which is only differentiated has independence with respect to his cognitive system.

In the reduction of initial uncertainty, some meaning no doubt has been ascribed, but such meaning is only of peripheral quality in relation to the total system or cognitive structure. This is because there are several important mediating steps which must be taken before newly admitted information can be integrated as interdependent subsystems in the entire cognitive structure. These steps include fidelity testing, pacing, expansion, and finally integration within the individual's fund of available and usable knowledge. Lacking these integrative steps, as, for example, when the learning strategy is simply the committing of new information to memory, the meaning content remains independent of possible usefulness beyond the point of simple recall. Such learning strategy leads to progressive segregation, increasing independence of subsystems, and greater concreteness characteristic of increasingly closed systems.

The example we have given concerns only one process in learning that an individual might utilize. But what about differentiation processes in that system we call a school? The analogy does not seem to break down because our attempts to have a school system produce a better behavior product often lead to greater independence of certain types of functions of people in the various subsystems of a school. For example, in the past five or six years there has been a rise of team teaching in the schools of the United States. This is an innovation frequently applied to minimize the adverse effects of increasing class size. Skillfully introduced and coordinated, team teaching can also bring out the main strengths of each teacher.

Let us assume that a principal is faced with the problem of differentiating, from available information, some means to modify the educational program in order to accommodate an overabundance of pupils, limited number of classrooms, and limited financial resources. If his habitual strategy is to differentiate only one or two attractive aspects of available information, he might arbitrarily adjust schedules and assign team responsibilities to certain teachers. If the staff lacks the information derived from faculty participation in the selection of alternatives, interaction in discussion, planning, and curriculum modification, the independence of such an innovation will restrict information flow and result in an increasingly closed system. Although relatively few administrators would take such ill-advised action, any independence of action which does not take into account all of the subsystems influenced by it and the probable changes in systems action will contribute to a breakdown of the systems' functioning.

We are inclined to take for granted the verbal discourse and general pattern of interaction between teachers and pupils in the classroom. All schools have in some manner made a distinction between "pupil" behavior and "teacher" behavior in the classroom. In other words, the roles of these two subsystems in the school have been differentiated, ostensibly for the purpose of having the behavior of both teacher and pupil become more precise and hopefully to produce more competent individuals. Each of the parties has some freedom in the way in which he will function in the school classroom. The abiding question, of course, is what kind of freedom and to what degree should the freedom be exercised? We have tried to make some suggestions along these lines in Chapters 5 and 6.

We have thought it proper to point out that teachers and pupils have some latitude in differentiating what their behavioral roles shall be in a classroom. It would seem equally logical that the principal should differentiate his administrative functions from all other functions of all other subsystems of the school. Should the administrative functions not be different from other parts of the system there would be difficulty in justifying the role of the principal. We hasten to add that there is no attempt here to suggest that the principal's role is not needed. Yet we do suggest that his actions be sufficiently different from other actions in the system we are calling the school so that he makes a unique contribution to the development of more competent teachers and pupils.

Now we pose a hypothetical question: How far can differentiation proceed in any subsystem of the school? Are there no limits? Theoretically, a subsystem could proceed so far toward independence that it no longer would remain a part of the system in which it originated. Hence, its exchange of information with other subsystems would be impossible. It would seem that there must be limits to prevent a subsystem from becoming differentiated to the point of becoming progressively segregated from the rest of the school. In this sense the teacher-pupil subsystem, the support subsystem, and the principal subsystem would no longer be integral yet differentiated parts of that total system we refer to as the school. These subsystems would bear so little relation and would contribute so little information to the other subsystems that one could say that they had progressively achieved, through independence, complete segregation. Indeed, if these subsystems each became so segregated from all of the other subsystems, then it would have to be said that the school was running down rather than up "the integration hill."

Differentiation in learning and freedom of subsystems are entirely desirable as long as the communication of information is sustained. Yet neither individual learning nor the functioning of a system can be said to be excellent if only the previously named processes are in operation.

Before concluding the discussion of differentiation, it should be pointed out that individuals as well as schools which habitually process information at this level may appear to be well integrated with their environment under conditions requiring the simple repetition of facts. Yet they are cognitive cripples under conditions requiring innovation or the practical use of highly abstract kinds of information. As information systems they become progressively static. Lacking the quality of interaction within their cognitive structure, they approach the state of a closed system.

When, on the other hand, differentiation leads to abstraction, interrelatedness, clarity and openness, there is free information exchange. Lacking concreteness, compartmentalization, ambiguity, and closedness, the system is adaptive and capable of making, and of responding to changes in the environment with increasing cognitive competence. This leads us to the second ego function discussed in Chapter 2, which seems to apply to the school and community as well as to the learning and mental health of an individual.

Fidelity and Adaptiveness

Before information may be incorporated at higher levels of integration and bring about more competent behavior, such information must be fairly consistent with beliefs and values already held. Fidelity testing is a mediating step in this process. Differentiation has been described as the way in which information from specific events, objects and relationships is separated one from another. Fidelity testing is the process of assimilating information into the cognitive structure with greater clarity and accuracy. To extend our analogy a bit, there is a counterpart of the ego process of fidelity testing that is embodied in the systems analysis approach.

One of the properties of a system is that it can be said to be adaptive when it changes in response to changes in the environment. We believe that not only is the system adaptive when it changes in response to environmental changes but that there is a very close relationship between the change that occurs in the systems action and the resulting change that occurs in the environment. This is the fidelity testing and adaptiveness factor.

A school that is really "in touch" with its environment, the community, is in the main serving the purpose for which it was created by that environment. By being in touch, we simply mean that there is a free flow of information among the various subsystems of the school and between the school and the social order in which it functions. It is highly likely that with this free flow of information there is less likelihood for the school as a total system to distort any negative information that comes to the school and has reference to the way the school is organized or the way it functions. Thus it can be said that this school assimilates the information with fidelity.

Of course, the converse applies as well, the less freely information flows among the subsystems, the greater is the likelihood that negative information about the school (which becomes known to the school) tends to be distorted. And with distortion there is less chance that the school as a total system will be able to make needed changes in its organization and in its functioning. To express this same idea in systems analysis terms, we can say that the system becomes less adaptive. The principle might be worded thus: with higher fidelity there is a corresponding higher degree of adaptiveness of the school; and the lower the fidelity (that is, distortion), the greater the probability that the school is nonadaptive. Two examples seem to be in order, one that illustrates the positive side of the fidelity-adaptive aspects; the other example highlighting the distortion-nonadaptive aspects of information flow.

School A is an elementary school located in a highly urban area. The parents of the school children were dropouts at the minimum legal school dropout age. In many ways the parents of the children who attend this school fit the description of the typically culturally disadvantaged person. Most notable of the behavioral traits of the parents and children of this school community are their grossly inadequate language abilities. The parents speak in short, incomplete, and grammatically incorrect sentences. Only a moment's conversation with them makes it clear that richness and depth are absent from their language, since they use practically no adverbs or adjectives. Equally obvious is that the repetitive use of conjunctions stitches together small fragments of thought. This is not unlike the very young child who, when telling a story, uses the conjunctions "and" or "then" in a repetitive and monotonous way.

Two major subsystems of the school, the administrative and the instructional, have advocated a curriculum content that emphasizes grammar, particularly as it is expressed in written language. There has been little attempt to involve another, and important, subsystem of the school in planning learning experiences. We refer to the school environment (community). With each school year it becomes increasingly clear to the administrative and instructional subsystems that the pupils are "retarded" because they do not learn to use the grammar that is expected of them and their attempts to write are abortive, to say the least. It is apparent that a certain kind of curriculum content in this school has been symbolized as having great learning value for the pupils. The fidelity of these symbols in relation to the behavior of both the pupils and their parents is low. Expressing this in the parlance of systems analysis, we can also say that this school is not adaptive, for it has not changed accurately in response to its environment.

School B is located in the same city as School A but on the other side of town, though the School B community is identical with that of School A. Rather early, the administrative and instructional subsystems of this school elected to emphasize curriculum content that highlighted grammar expressed in written form. Before long the teachers became aware that the children were not learning what they were expected to learn. The children were apathetic toward grammar in written form, even though they tried to learn it. In this sense the pupils can be said to have transmitted information to their teachers. In turn, these teachers made the information known to the principal. The principal quickly arranged some meetings between parents of the community, teachers and himself.

Out of these conferences grew a plan whereby the pupils were given many opportunities for direct experience through taking many field trips. On their return to the classroom after the field trips, the teacher was careful to have the children discuss what they had seen as well as their attitudes about what they had observed. In contrast to a curriculum that emphasized grammar and written expression, this curriculum emphasized direct experiencing and verbal expression.

In the case of School B, it can be said that the symbols or meanings which had been attached to a certain kind of curriculum content and instructional procedure were not bound too tightly. Therefore it became possible to change the curriculum content after there had been exchange of information among the various subsystems of the school. This school can be said to be adaptive, for it not only changed in response to its environment, but there was high fidelity between the information received and the meaning that had been attached to it.

Pacing and Stability

We have said that a stable system is one that keeps its internal functions in a steady state. This implies the quality of flexibility, along with the capacity to manage varying amounts of information input without overloading the system function either in terms of quality or quantity. Considering the pacing function of the ego or a school, it is reasonable to believe that there are input limits above which its internal functioning would be hampered and that output would tend to diminish in quantity and/or quality. Pacing is a selective function, since it protects the system from overloading or "being jammed" by information in too great a volume, or at rates less than those at which the system functions most effectively. In other words, pacing implies a dearth as well as a surplus of information input.

As we consider ways in which a system seeking to maintain a steady state modifies its action to cope with environmental input stimuli, we are concerned also with ways in which the system might introduce environmental changes more congruent with its needs. Information drawn from a given object or event might be appraised in terms of the extent to which the information was viewed as deviating from one's expectancies. Thus individuals might behave quite differently. Upon receipt of what is presumed to be the same information, one having no previous knowledge and therefore no concept of the meaning of the information, might exhibit no change in behavior. Another, already in possession of the information, might perceive it as redundant and behave in a similar manner. Still another individual might perceive the information as ambiguous and simply compartmentalize the information for recall. An individual, already under stress, might find the information input threatening and intolerable in terms of his ability to manage new input. In the last case, the variation from expectancy might be referred to as "noise," since it would serve only to aggravate an already overloaded system.

We have already commented on the school as a system that must of necessity develop functions that are closely related to and are even an outgrowth of some environmental conditions. The example used was that of establishing a language program for culturally disadvantaged children. This all sounds well and good, but as any principal or supervisor knows, there are hundreds of environmental changes that could, conceivably, be incorporated into a school's program. There must be limits to this process. Even though the society in which a school functions may have many different kinds of needs which the school could help to satisfy, there is a factor of *pacing* to be considered.

Let us suppose that an elementary school located in a rural farming community suddenly finds that a mammoth high-rise apartment development is built adjacent to the school. Many principals will recognize this as a common occurrence. With the completion of construction there comes a multitude of children with special learning needs. Thus, we see in our hypothetical situation that the school suddenly finds itself with gifted children, retarded children, speech handicapped children, disturbed children, those children wanting a foreign language in the elementary school program, demands for creative writing, and great expressions of interest in drama, art and music. However, let us not confuse the issue, the question is not *whether* the school should begin various activities and programs; rather, it is a question of how many such activities and programs can be started at once and still have the school remain as a stable, viable system.

It is true that any school must differentiate its program and its activities with fidelity; yet we are now concerned with the rate of assimilation (pacing) of these activities or programs into the total functioning of the school. To put it differently, pacing has to do with the way in which the school changes its structure (organization) and its function (teaching and curriculum development) as the environment changes. If this hypothetical school were to try to put immediately into practice all of the different programs needed to take care of those new learner needs and interests, already expressed, it would in effect overload itself.

A good analogy to this situation is that of the youngster who is taken on a whirlwind-sightseeing tour of some famous historical place. In a brief period of time, he is exposed to a great number of new and varied stimuli. At the conclusion of the trip, the youngster is frequently unable to describe or report what he saw or learned with the exception of a few outstanding incidents. Often he remembers only his fatigue and the feeling of being coerced by the pressure of the itinerary. This example, again, indicates the factor of overloading.

Of course, one can always point to the opposite condition from that which we have just described. That is, a school does not remain stable in the sense of keeping all of its internal functions in equilibrium (programming to help children learn better). To go back to the example of the rural school which has suddenly had an influx of students, we have said that the whole school would be "jammed" if it tried simultaneously to incorporate all the programs and conditions mentioned. However, the school could not hope to remain as a stable system if it did not initiate *some* of the programs. This is true because, if the needs of the pupils (a subsystem) were not being satisfied, no significant learning would occur and the system as a whole would be seriously disadvantaged. What this means, then, is that the school operates well when there is a certain pacing applied to the change in function of all the subsystems of the school. It is worth repeating that pacing is a concept that applies both to too rapid change and to change that proceeds too slowly.

Expansion and Hierarchial Order

Expansion implies the development of a system through a series of steps toward a state of hierarchial ordering in which the relationship of all subsystems are interdependent along a gradation from the least significant to the most significant. When all entities within the cognitive structure have been aligned in hierarchial order, including "self," the individual has achieved a level of integration enabling him to make valid judgments relative to objects and situations in his environment. Through the process of expansion, he becomes increasingly sensitive to relevant or irrelevant information with respect to his goals. His awareness of pertinent detail concerning situations and events becomes increasingly acute.

As we stated earlier, even open systems have within them the capacity for degeneration. The ego as an information processing system will degenerate when constriction replaces expansion. Degeneration occurs in a system when the free flow and control of information to all interdependent subsystems no longer is possible. The degenerate system tends toward closedness and rigidity. Creativity, imagination, purpose, improvisation and invention are unlikely where sensitivity to environmental change is lacking. An individual under these circumstances will become progressively incapable of maintaining a repertoire of socially appropriate behavior.

Anyone who has had even a modicum of experience with schools knows that in an implicit or explicit way schools have a "point of view." This point of view seems to be the "glue" that binds a school together and gives it a sense of purpose and perhaps even a sense of destiny. In some schools a point of view comes about primarily because of the accumulation of experience. That is to say, as the years go by there evolves an implicit, sometimes vague, but functionally real point of view. In other schools this so-called point of view was formulated at the time the school was first opened. An administrator may have felt that it was modish to have a philosophy, which once written was filed away and never used again. In still other schools the point of view is considered, at least in part, at each weekly faculty meeting.

This point of view is comprised of value judgments about who engages in curriculum development and for what purposes; about teacher-pupil relationships; about the way in which learning and motivation are facilitated; and about the way in which the administration functions in such a way as to expedite all of the above. Yet what is equally important is that these value judgments are arranged in a hierarchy with some things being more important than others. The determination of what is important comes about as a result of the flow of information from the various subsystems of the school (community, teachers, pupils and administrator). In short there is flow of information, the information is synthesized so as to produce symbols, and these symbols have a certain loading, i.e., they are arranged in a priority order.

If information continues to flow within the subsystems, then it is likely that the symbols themselves will become altered as time transpires. To put it simply, the point of view of the school will be slowly expanding or growing. If information does not flow freely, then the point of view is unchanging and even constricted. The change will not occur simply because some new technique of grouping has been devised, or a new instructional medium invented, or the school caught on the ground swell of a fad. The important principle is that, just as an individual learner can bind and unbind symbols in his symbolic repertoire, so can the school. And as the school takes on these new symbols as a result of binding and unbinding, it is able to assimilate new information and to arrange the new information in its proper place in the hierarchy.

Some schools are obviously more vital systems than others. This becomes quickly apparent after only a relatively few moments in a school. It does not take long to learn that some schools are performing primarily a "custodial" function. If one were to change the clothing on teachers and pupils, make some slight changes in the instructional materials and architecture of the building, then such a school would be exactly what it was a century ago. Teachers in these schools perceive themselves as "going no place" either as persons or as professionals. In such a school it can be expected that there would be high teacher turnover. It can likewise be expected that those teachers who remain are the ones less likely to have a beneficial effect on pupils' learning. Usually this feeling of "going no place" results from the fact that this system which we are calling a school has not derived symbols, concepts or metaphors concerning a number of basic things, such as: what the school's role is as an institution; what the teacher's role is in such a school; and the relationship between the subject matter taught by the teachers and the learning of pupils. In addition, there is a growing dislike on the part of the various people in the subsystems to think about any of the above. The people, the subsystems of the school, have bound symbols in such a rigid way that such a school is frozen and incapable of change. Just as a frozen pipe is incapable of transmitting a fluid, so is a school that is symbolically frozen incapable of transmitting information to pupils in such a way as to help them become competent persons.

When a school tends toward openness, the expansion of existing subsystems makes growth possible. We have in mind, here, growth in effective communication of information. For example, the support services subsystem representing, among others, the school psychologist, social worker and counselor customarily provides remedial kinds of services by working intensively with individual pupils referred by teachers. Pupils so considered often fail to measure up to standards of achievement in school subjects or in social competence. Although this is a highly desirable, necessary and successful kind of service, the intensive study of the pupil in his environment, coupled with case conferences and written reports, is of necessity limited to a few of the more seriously handicapped pupils. Unfortunately, there are not enough people engaged in support services to meet in the traditional ways the need for these services. The need for remediation is evident from kindergarten through college even though we use an example of "primary prevention" from the elementary school.

The current practice of introducing counselors into elementary schools can prove to be an expansion of support services by linking existing subsystems into new relationships. In this case, primary prevention puts emphasis on the act of teaching. This is a way of utilizing specialized professional insights to provide teachers a great deal more information about individual differences and ways in which these may be met. Primary prevention is a way of picking up information communicated by pupils through a variety of behaviors. In order to receive this information with fidelity, the teacher must be a fairly sensitive diagnostician. Equally important, teachers must achieve greater skill in pulling together information which makes sense to them in teaching pupils. Here is where the support service consultant can be of increasing value. One way is through the seminar approach in which the pupil behavior specialist helps teachers to differentiate meaningful behavior information and to incorporate this into teaching methodology in the classroom. Such a procedure could become the core of teacher in-service education programs within the school.

Integration and Wholeness

The cognitive structure can become so thoroughly compartmentalized that there seems to be little relationship between what an individual comprehends and what he does. Integration is the unifying force which permeates both the subjective and objective realms of the cognitive field, establishing pathways of communication over which meaning can travel. This brings about greater wholeness and openness which make possible an increasing capacity for adaptation as the system encounters environmental change.

If we think of the cognitive field as the map of a city, integration would be represented by the streets, alleys, freeways, railways, and air corridors over which "meaning traffic" is routed on its way to a tentative destination. In more concrete terms, the channels of communication between school and community as well as the in-school modes of communication are the corridors over which information is routed. Examples of the former are: parent-teacher conferences, report cards, home visits, and case conferences. Types of in-school communication are: the teaching of subject matter, praise and criticism by teachers, faculty meetings, and posted rules and regulations.

Integrative processes are also in need of constant maintenance and repair as they are widened and extended to facilitate communication in newly differentiated areas of knowing and behaving. As progressive systemization occurs in the process of growth, the freeways and byways are paved with experience to expedite the flow of traffic to and from the inner and outer worlds. From time to time, as channels of communication are blocked and congested by overloading, integrative processes establish detours to relieve congestion until repairs have been completed. Each individual becomes his own engineer as he learns to cope with real problems in his environment. But he does not work alone. He is supervised and guided by a board of commissioners representing society, who both facilitate and limit his style of development, requiring him to modify his blueprint consistent with their expectations.

Previously we discussed the way in which the point of view of a school is formulated by binding of symbols, and the way it is modified by unbinding those symbols as information flows through the school's subsystems. Yet it seems possible that this could happen and the behavior of pupils, teachers and parents would not be affected in the slightest. In short, the symbolic repertoire of the school must have accompanying channels or means by which individuals can express themselves relative to the symbols.

A symbol (meaning) is an abstraction and must not ever be confused with operation. For example, a school might well, through the expansion processes mentioned previously, crystalize or symbolize a new statement having to do with teacher-pupil relationships. But this does not help the teacher to know how he should behave, nor does it help pupils and parents to know how they should act. Thus, the symbol "teacher-pupil relationships" should never be confused with the teacher putting his arm around a child's shoulder or a student being impertinent to a teacher. The latter is the real thing, while the former is the way it has been symbolized.

The metaphors or concepts (symbols) a school subscribes to must be integrated into the different "layers" (subsystems) of the school. This occurs at the behavioral level. The people in the subsystems must *act* differently after new concepts or metaphors have been developed in the school. However, each person will act uniquely differently than others. By acting uniquely differently, even though subscribing to a given concept, people in the subsystems are helping the system to move toward wholeness. We might also say that the school is moving in the direction of becoming progressively systematized.

In summary, in this chapter we have tried to create an analogy between the ego mediation processes employed by a pupil while learning, and certain processes the school uses to organize and modify its program. The latter processes are ones derived from the relatively new field of operation called systems analysis. In short, we have pointed out how ego mediation processes have counterpart properties in a system. Yet our purpose was not merely to engage in the intellectual exercise of creating an analogy; rather, we endeavored to present a unique way of viewing and appraising a school.

There are those, of course, who will quarrel with the modified systems analysis approach we have suggested. They would argue that the systems approach did not arise from within education and, therefore, has no relevance to it. Our rejoinder is that systems analysis has to do with the flow of information in an organization. One does not have to be clairvoyant to recognize that the stock-in-trade of education is information. The curriculum is a body of information; the admonitions of teachers to pupils are information; the administrative regulations of the principal are information; and the content of parents' communications with the school is information.

In order to live effectively in today's world, a person must have adequate information. The same can be said of a school, but there must also be a free flow and control of information in that school. Thus, we have held that the systems analysis approach, with appropriate modification, holds promise for use in the schools of the nation.

Bibliography

1. Robert M. Gagne. *Psychological Principles in Systems Development*. New York: Holt, Rinehart & Winston, 1962.
2. A. D. Hall and R. E. Fagen. "Definition of a System." *General Systems* Vol. 1, 1956.
3. O. J. Harvey, David E. Hunt and Harold M. Schroder. *Conceptual Systems and Personality Organization*. New York: John Wiley & Sons, Inc., 1961.
4. Robert F. Mager. *Preparing Instructional Objectives*. San Francisco, California: Fearon Publishing Co., Inc., 1962.
5. James G. Miller. "Information Overload." *Self-Organizing Systems*. M. C. Yovits, editor. Washington, D.C.: Spartan Books, Inc., 1962.
6. George Gaylord Simpson. *This View of Life*. New York: Harcourt, Brace & World, 1964.

The ASCD 1966 Yearbook Committee and Contributors

Walter B. Waetjen, *Chairman*
   Assistant to the President for Administrative Affairs, University of Maryland, College Park, Maryland
Eli M. Bower
   Consultant, Mental Health in Education, Community Research and Services Branch, National Institute of Mental Health, Rockville, Maryland
Elizabeth M. Drews
   Associate Professor, College of Education, Michigan State University, East Lansing, Michigan
Robert S. Fleming
   Assistant Commissioner of Education, State of New Jersey Department of Education, Trenton, New Jersey
Ira J. Gordon
   Professor, College of Education, University of Florida, Gainesville, Florida
Marie M. Hughes
   Professor, College of Education, University of Arizona, Tucson, Arizona
James Raths
   Associate Professor, Bureau of Educational Research and Field Services, University of Maryland, College Park, Maryland
Donald Snygg
   Chairman, Department of Psychology, State University College, Oswego, New York
Kenneth C. Weisbrod
   Associate Dean, Counseling and Testing Division, California State College, Long Beach, California

ASCD Board of Directors

As of November 1, 1965

Executive Committee, 1965-66

President, Galen Saylor, Chairman, Department of Secondary Education, Teachers College, University of Nebraska, Lincoln.
President-Elect, Arthur W. Combs, Professor of Education, University of Florida, Gainesville.
Vice-President, Harold D. Drummond, Chairman, Department of Elementary Education, University of New Mexico, Albuquerque.
Vernon E. Anderson, Dean and Professor, College of Education, University of Maryland, College Park.
Dorris May Lee, Professor of Education, Portland State College, Portland, Oregon.
Gertrude M. Lewis, Specialist for Upper Grades, Office of Education, U.S. Department of Health, Education, and Welfare, Washington, D.C.
Sybil K. Richardson, Professor of Education, San Fernando Valley State College, Northridge, California.

Members Elected at Large

Melvin W. Barnes, Pub. Schs., Portland, Ore. (1967); Herbert I. Bruning, Pub. Schs., Shawnee Mission, Kan. (1968); Arthur W. Combs, Univ. of Fla., Gainesville (1967); Muriel Crosby, Pub. Schs., Wilmington, Del. (1967); Harold D. Drummond, Univ. of N. Mex., Albuquerque (1966); Mrs. Minnie H. Fields, Fla. St. Dept. of Ed., Tallahassee (1969); Ned A. Flanders, Univ. of Mich., Ann Arbor (1969); Robert S. Fox, Univ. of Mich., Ann Arbor (1967); Richard A. Gibboney, St. Dept. of Pub. Instr., Harrisburg, Pa. (1968); Anne Gustafson, Pub. Schs., Rockford, Ill. (1967); Mrs. Marie Hughes, Univ. of Ariz., Tucson

(1966); Victor B. Lawhead, Ball St. Tchrs. Coll., Muncie, Ind. (1968); Helen K. Mackintosh, U.S. Office of Ed., Wash., D.C. (1969); M. Karl Openshaw, Ohio St. Univ., Columbus (1969); Mrs. Claudia B. Pitts, Arlington Co. Schs., Arlington, Va. (1966); Chandos Reid, Pub. Schs., Pontiac, Mich. (1966); Lola Toler, Pub. Schs., Tulsa, Okla. (1968); Walter B. Waetjen, Univ. of Md., College Park (1966); Hugh B. Wood, Tongue Point Job Corps Cntr., Astoria, Ore. (1969).

State Representatives to the Board

Alabama—Robert Bills, Univ. of Ala., University; Robert C. Hatch, Ala. Ldrshp. Devel. Prog., Montgomery; John T. Lovell, Auburn Univ., Auburn. *Arizona*—James J. Jelinek, Ariz. St. Univ., Tempe; Herbert Wilson, Univ. of Ariz., Tucson; Louise Withers, Pub. Schs., Monterey Park. *Arkansas*—Wallace C. Floyd, Pub. Schs., Ft. Smith; Joe J. Slaven, Pub. Schs., Fayetteville. *California*—Richard L. Foster, Pub. Schs., Danville; Barbara Hartsig, Calif. St. Coll. at Fullerton, Fullerton; Mary B. Lane, San Francisco St. Coll., San Francisco; Mrs. Mary H. Mitchell, Pub. Schs., Palm Springs; Mrs. Mary S. Reed, Pub. Schs., El Segundo; Sybil K. Richardson, San Fernando Valley St. Coll., Northridge. *Colorado*—Eugene R. Gullette, Pub. Schs., Boulder; Rolland Walters, Pub. Schs., Englewood. *Dakota (North and South)*—Robert D. Benton, Pub. Schs., Rapid City, S. Dak.; John Yourd, Pub. Schs., Fargo, N. Dak. *Delaware*—George V. Kirk, Pub. Schs., Newark; Melville F. Warren, Pub. Schs., Dover. *District of Columbia*—Wendell A. Parris, Pub. Schs., Wash., D.C.; LuVerne C. Walker, Pub. Schs., Wash., D.C. *Florida*—Mrs. Marian W. Black, Fla. St. Univ., Tallahassee; E. L. Bowers, Escambia Co. Schs., Pensacola; Joseph W. Crenshaw, St. Dept. of Ed., Tallahassee; John McIntyre, Dade Co. Schs., Miami; Sam H. Moorer, St. Dept. of Ed., Tallahassee; Rodney Nowakowski, Dade Co. Schs., Perrine. *Georgia*—Johnnye V. Cox, Univ. of Ga., Athens; Mrs. Edith E. Grimsley, Bibb Co. Schs., Macon; John Lounsbury, Ga. St. Coll. for Women, Milledgeville; Lester D. Stephens, Univ. of Ga., Athens. *Hawaii*—Ernest J. Cherry, Hawaii Dept. of Ed., Honolulu; Billie Hollingshead, Church Coll. of Hawaii, Laie, Oahu. *Idaho*—Doris Hoyer, Pub. Schs., Boise; Doyle Lowder, Pub. Schs., Rupert. *Illinois*—Earl Dieken, Pub. Schs., Glen Ellyn; Edith Ford, Pub. Schs., Park Ridge; Cecilia J. Lauby, Ill. St. Normal Univ., Normal; Urey Robertson, Pub. Schs., Herrin; J. Harlan Shores, Univ. of Ill., Urbana; Theodore R. Storlie, Pub. Schs., Flossmoor. *Indiana*—Mrs. Mary Castle, Marion Co. Schs., Indianapolis; LaVelle Fortenberry, Ind. Univ., Gary Center, Gary; Lewis Gilfoy, Pub. Schs., Indianapolis; Frank Hunter, Perry Twp. Schs., Indianapolis. *Iowa*—Gladys H. Horgen, St. Dept. of Ed., Des Moines; Mildred Middleton, Pub. Schs., Cedar Rapids; Mrs. Mable Root, Pub. Schs., Des Moines. *Kansas*—Mrs. Perva Hughes, Kansas St. Coll., Pittsburg; J. Harvey Littrell, Kansas St. Univ., Manhattan; Melvin L. Winters, Pub. Schs., Kansas City. *Kentucky*—Grace Champion, Pub. Schs., Louisville; Mrs. Alice C. Harned, Bullitt Co. Schs., Shepherdsville; Mrs. Mary S. Marshall, Ky. St. Dept. of Ed., Frankfort. *Louisiana*—John D. Greene, East Baton Rouge Parish Sch. Bd., Baton Rouge; Mary Lou Loudon, Pub. Schs.,

Baton Rouge; Gaither McConnell, Tulane Univ., New Orleans; Beverly L. White, St. James Parish Sch. Bd., Lutcher. *Maryland*—G. Alfred Helwig, Baltimore Co. Bd. of Ed., Towson; Norman J. Moore, Cecil Co. Bd. of Ed., Elkton; Louise F. Thompson, Bd. of Ed., Frederick; Fred G. Usilton, Caroline Co. Bd. of Ed., Denton. *Michigan*—Charles A. Blackman, Mich. St. Univ., East Lansing; Wendell Hough, Jr., Wayne St. Univ., Detroit; Alvin D. Loving, Univ. of Mich., Ann Arbor; Dorothy McCuskey, Western Mich. Univ., Kalamazoo; M. Wilmer Menge, Wayne St. Univ., Detroit; William C. Miller, Wayne Co. Sch. Dist., Detroit. *Minnesota*—S. A. Christian, Pub. Schs., Rochester; A. E. Edstrom, Pub. Schs., Hopkins; Josephine Kremer, Pub. Schs., Austin. *Missouri*—Mark Lumb, Pub. Schs., Brentwood; Jack E. Morris, Pub. Schs., Ferguson; Homer Willis, Pub. Schs., Louisiana. *Montana*—A. G. Erickson, Pub. Schs., Helena; Winston E. Weaver, Pub. Schs., Billings. *Nebraska*—George W. Bailey, Pub. Schs., Bellevue; Maria Laas, Westside Community Schs., Omaha. *Nevada*—Monty Boland, Pub. Schs., Henderson; Mrs. Rose Bullis, Pub. Schs., Reno. *New Jersey*—Marion W. Fox, Atlantic City; Robert S. Fleming, St. Dept. of Ed., Trenton; Malcolm Katz, Pub. Schs., Ridgewood; Bernard Packin, Pub. Schs., Parsippany; Robert S. Ward, St. Dept. of Ed., Trenton. *New Mexico*—Ralph Drake, Pub. Schs., Portales; James C. Porterfield, Gallup-McKinley Co. Schs., Gallup. *New York*—Mrs. Lillian T. Brooks, Pub. Schs., Rochester; Gerald A. Cleveland, Pub. Schs., Syracuse; John E. Owens, Pub. Schs., Roslyn; O. Ward Satterlee, St. Univ. Coll., Potsdam; *North Carolina*—Annie Lee Jones, Univ. of N.C., Chapel Hill; Douglas R. Jones, East Carolina Coll., Greenville; Robert C. Hanes, Pub. Schs., Charlotte; Melvin Stahl, Guilford Co. Schs., Greensboro. *Ohio*—Howard Brown, Pub. Schs., Springfield; O. L. Davis, Jr., Kent St. Univ., Kent; Lloyd W. Dull, Pub. Schs., Canton; Martha L. King, Ohio St. Univ., Columbus; Mrs. Audrey Norris, Univ. of Cinci., Cincinnati; Hilda Stocker, Pub. Schs., Brecksville. *Oklahoma*—Mrs. Frances Curb, Pub. Schs., Lawton; Helen M. Jones, Okla. St. Univ., Stillwater. *Oregon*—Alma Irene Bingham, Portland St. Coll., Portland; George Henderson, Pub. Schs., Lebanon; Lloyd F. Millhollen, Jr., Pub. Schs., Eugene; Melvin F. Moore, Pub. Schs., Eugene; Helen E. Schaper, Pub. Schs., Portland. *Pennsylvania*—Richard De Remer, Univ. of Pittsburgh, Pittsburgh; Margaret McFeaters, Slippery Rock St. Coll., Slippery Rock; Gerald M. Newton, Beaver Co. Pub. Schs., Beaver; William W. Oswalt, Lehigh Co. Pub. Schs., Allentown; Elwood L. Prestwood, Lower Merion Twp. Schs., Ardmore. *Puerto Rico*—Mrs. Awilda Aponte de Saldaña. Univ. of Puerto Rico, Rió Piedras; Mrs. Ana D. Soto, Univ. of Puerto Rico, Rió Piedras. *South Carolina*—Ray Miley, Pub. Schs., Greenville; Howard Moody, Pub. Schs., Conway. *Tennessee*—Emily Beebe, Pub. Schs., Memphis; Will Bowdoin, Middle Tenn. St. Coll., Murfreesboro; Mrs. Elizabeth L. Dalton, Univ. of Chattanooga, Chattanooga. *Texas*—Joe A. Airola, Spring Branch Pub. Schs., Houston; Alma M. Freeland, Univ. of Texas, Austin; Mrs. Caroline Locke, Pub. Schs., Fort Worth; Mrs. Bernice H. Railsback, Pub. Schs., Levelland; Margaret Wasson, Highland Park Independent Sch. Dist., Dallas. *Utah*—James O. Morton, Pub.

Schs., Salt Lake City. *Virginia*—Virginia Benson, Pub. Schs., Fairfax; Evelyn L. Berry, Pub. Schs., Petersburg; R. Beatrice Bland, Longwood Coll., Farmville; Julian B. Dunn, Pub. Schs., Williamsburg. *Washington*—John Amend, Tacoma-Pierce Co. Opportunity and Devel., Inc., Tacoma; Mrs. Ellen Herminhaus, Pierce Co. Schs., Tacoma; Arthur Lind, Pub. Schs., Richland. *West Virginia*—Mabel Dick, Kanawha Co. Schs., Charleston. *Wisconsin*—Eugene Balts, Pub. Schs., Oshkosh; Burdett Eagon, Wis. St. Coll., Stevens Point; Fred Overman, Dept. of Pub. Instr., Madison; Doris G. Phipps, Pub. Schs., Sheboygan. *Wyoming*—F. Robert Ellison, Pub. Schs., Casper; Clarence L. Ward, Pub. Schs., Torrington. *New England (Connecticut, Maine, Massachusetts, New Hampshire, Rhode Island, Vermont)*—John Economopoulos, St. Dept. of Ed., Concord, N.H.; Priscilla Ferguson, Pub. Schs., Portland, Maine; Ruth Johnson, Pub. Schs., Portland, Maine; L. Gertrude Lawrence, Pub. Schs., Wethersfield, Conn., Ruth E. Mayo, Pub. Schs., Stoneham, Mass.

ASCD Headquarters Staff

Executive Secretary: Leslee J. Bishop
Associate Secretary; Editor, ASCD Publications: Robert R. Leeper
Associate Secretaries: Robert J. Alfonso, Louise M. Berman
Washington Intern: Benjamin P. Ebersole
Administrative Assistant: Virginia Berthy
Staff Assistants:

Sarah Arlington
Penny Artwohl
Betty Lou Atkins
Susan G. Atkinson
C. Deborah Barker
Ruth P. Ely
Karen L. Farr

Ruby J. Funkhouser
Marie K. Haut
Velez G. Hilton
Teola T. Jones
Suzanne Lang
Frances Mindel
Kathleen Vail